W9-CDW-752

EXTRAORDINARY WOMEN JOURNALISTS

EXTRAORDINARY

WOMEN

JOURNALISTS

by

Claire Price-Groff

Children's Press®

A Division of Grolier Publishing

New York London Hong Kong Sydney

Danbury, Connecticut

Dedication

To Howard . . .

Acknowledgments

The author would like to thank Helen Gurley Brown, Georgie Ann Geyer, Mary McGrory, Katharine Graham, and the late Erma Bombeck for their kind and gracious assistance in preparing this book. The author would also like to thank her husband for his patience in reading several preliminary drafts of the book and her writing friends who helped her to polish the rough drafts into their final form. A very special thank-you is due to Mark Friedman, who agreed with the author that this was a book worthy of being written.

Library of Congress Cataloging-in-Publication Data

Price-Groff, Claire.

Extraordinary women journalists / by Claire Price-Groff.

p. cm. — (Extraordinary people)

Includes bibliographical references and index.

Summary: Profiles the life and work of notable women journalists, including Sarah Hale, Margaret Fuller, and Nellie Bly.

ISBN 0-516-20474-2 (lib. bdg.)   0-516-26242-4 (pbk.)

1. Women journalists—Biography—Juvenile literature. [1. Journalists.] I. Title.   II. Series.

PN4820.P75   1997

070'.82—dc21

[B]

96-50341

CIP

AC

Contents

63
MIRIAM (FRANK) FLORENCE
FOLLINE LESLIE
1836–1914
Publisher, Editor

79
GERTRUDE BUSTILL MOSSELL
(N. F. MOSSELL)
1855–1948
Journalist, Feminist, Educator

96
AFRICAN-AMERICAN
WOMEN'S VOICES
IN JOURNALISM

67
VICTORIA C. WOODHULL
1838–1927
Reformer, Orator, Journalist

82
IDA MINERVA TARBELL
1857–1944
Journalist, Biographer, Lecturer

101
ELIZABETH COCHRANE
(NELLIE BLY)
1865–1922
Journalist, World Traveler

72
KATE FIELD
1858–1896
Journalist, Author, Lecturer,
Actress

86
ELIZABETH MERIWETHER
GILMER (DOROTHY DIX)
1861–1951
Crime Reporter and Advice Columnist

107
RHETA CHILDE DORR
1866–1948
Reporter, War Correspondent,
Feminist

75
ELIZA JANE POITEVENT
HOLBROOK NICHOLSON
1849–1896
Publisher, Poet

90
IDA B. WELLS-BARNETT
1862–1931
Journalist, Reformer

112
ANNE O'HARE MCCORMICK
1880–1954
Editorial Columnist and
Reporter

Preface

Why a book about women journalists? Because so few of these women have been publicly recognized for their accomplishments. Because, through their writing, so many of these women have been instrumental in helping to change society. And, because, as author of this book, I have a tremendous admiration for these women.

When I first thought about writing a book on women journalists, I planned to cover maybe eight or ten women. I read dozens of biographies and hundreds of profiles. I read books about American history and books about journalism. What I thought at first would be an easy task turned out to be a very difficult one. How could I choose eight or ten out of so many? Even when I expanded my scope, making the choices still seemed impossible.

"Wait a minute," I told myself. "You're not going to write about *all* women journalists. You're only going to write about the extraordinary ones."

I was faced with a new set of questions. What makes a person extraordinary? To be extraordinary means to be exceptional, to stand out from others, to be extra-special. Do exceptional people share certain qualities? Can one set out to become extraordinary, or is one simply born with that capacity?

I discovered that some of these women did, indeed, seem destined to become extraordinary—they came from families where the extraordinary was considered ordinary, and they lived up to the high expectations placed upon them by their parents. Others did not think of themselves as extraordinary, but were faced with extraordinary circumstances.

I discovered that there is no single definition of "extraordinary." Each woman profiled in this book is extraordinary in her own way. In reading about them, you will meet women who came from wealthy families and women who came from poor families. You will meet women whose education was limited and women who had advanced degrees. You will meet women who grew up in healthy, intact families and women who survived broken homes.

Yet, as different from one another as the women were, certain things do seem to stand out. Many of the women came from educated families and were exposed to books and ideas very early. Several of them came from families where independent thinking and creativity were fostered. As children, they were encouraged to be unafraid to be different from their peers. Other things stand out as well. Many of these women lost one or both of their parents at an early age. And of those who grew up with both parents, many seem to have had an exceptionally close relationship with their fathers—rather than with their mothers.

Some common personality traits also stand out in many of these women. They were challenged instead of frightened or put off by obstacles. They were stubborn, persistent, and refused to take "no" for an answer when they wanted something. They were unwilling to accept limits imposed on them by society or by other people.

My one regret in writing this book was that many extraordinary women journalists could not be included. Choosing from among women who wrote in the early periods of our history proved a somewhat less difficult task than choosing from among those who came later. Why? Simply because any woman who became a journalist in the eighteenth and nineteenth centuries was extraordinary. These were the women who helped pave the way for those who came later. Once I reached the twentieth century, my task became harder because so many more women were accepted as journalists. And the closer I came to the present day, my choices were ever more painful. But this is good! The numbers of women journalists today are so vast, it is impossible to choose only a few and say they are the extraordinary ones. I apologize for the many whose stories I have not included. The women I chose represent hundreds of others.

For girls and young women who dream of being journalists, the path has been made a little easier by the women described in this book. But remember that there are still new paths to open and unimagined battles to fight.

I end with one last thought for those readers who are considering making journalism their profession. Remember this: You can overcome whatever obstacles are placed in your path, just as your predecessors overcame the obstacles placed in theirs.

—— *Claire Price-Groff*

Women Printers and Publishers in Colonial America

It was by means of Newspapers that we received and spread the Notice of tyrannical Designs formed against America and kindled a Spirit that has been sufficient to repel them.

—JOHN HOLT, 1776

A proclamation from the governor by order of the king.

A ship arriving from England carrying eagerly awaited supplies needed for daily life.

The marriage or death of an important citizen.

All of these events were news. In the earliest days of the North American colonies, the only way this news could be broadcast was through a town crier or personal announcement. But this changed in 1638, when a Mistress Glover arrived in Boston with the first printing press in North America. She had left England with her husband, who died during the long sea voyage. Mistress Glover carried out his plans and established a print shop in Cambridge, Massachusetts. Thus, the very first printing press in America was owned by a woman.

Like other colonial printers who followed, Mistress Glover's shop printed advertisements, pamphlets, legal and business forms, almanacs, and prayer books. Occasionally she printed broadsides to announce special events and important news. Broadsides were large sheets of paper printed with news that were hung in public for people to read. As the colonies grew, the occasional broadsides evolved into weekly publications. Printers became publishers, editors, and writers, as well as typesetters and compositors. These early newspapers contained four pages filled with local news and letters from readers, stories reprinted from other papers, and advertisements. Like today, these advertisements provided a major source of income to the printer.

Most colonial print shops were owned by men, but often their wives, daughters, or sisters helped to run the business. Many of these women continued publishing when the man died. By the start of the Revolutionary War in 1775, there were at least fourteen women printers/publishers in the colonies.

Publishing a colonial newspaper was no easy task, especially for a woman. First, she had to write the stories with her quill pen. She had to choose and proofread which stories to use from other writers. Announcements and advertisements had to be collected. When she decided on all of an issue's contents, she laid out one page at a time and hand-cut the paper. Then, she did the typesetting by placing every metal letter of every word into a composing stick, which had to be inked. In warm weather, the ink might be too runny, and in the winter, both the ink and the paper might freeze. The entire process was a slow, tedious, messy job. On average, it took four days to prepare a four-page paper. Finally, the publisher had to turn the hand-crank to run the press. Once printed and dried, she would place the papers out for sale.

In addition to writing the stories and producing the newspaper, the printer solicited subscribers and advertisers and then collected the money they owed her. Of course, a woman printer also ran her household — preparing food, making soap and candles, sewing clothing, and taking care of her young children.

As trouble erupted between the colonies and England, those women who supported American independence put themselves at great personal risk by using their papers to speak out. Some, like Margaret Draper of Massachusetts remained loyal to the king of England and put themselves in danger by incurring the anger of the patriots. After the war, fearing for

Benjamin Franklin (left) working in a colonial-era print shop

her life, Draper fled to Nova Scotia and later to England. Others who supported the cause of freedom wrote editorials pointing out the king's repressive policies. These patriots printed excerpts from Tom Paine's famous pamphlets (as well as the pamphlets themselves) calling for independence. When the struggle erupted into war, the printers kept their readers informed of the war's progress and urged their readers to help the cause.

One of the first women to publish in the colonies was Elizabeth Timothy, who was born and raised in Holland and emigrated to America in 1731 with her husband Lewis and their four children. Shortly after their arrival in Philadelphia, the Timothys agreed to purchase the *Gazette* from Benjamin Franklin. For five years, Elizabeth ran the household and raised their children. In 1738, when Lewis died, Elizabeth kept the business going until her son Peter was old enough to take over in 1746. Elizabeth then opened a bookstore and stationery shop next door.

Elizabeth Timothy had a much better knack for business than her husband. Because he was slow in collecting money owed him, his payments to Franklin were often late. But when Elizabeth took over, she refused to accept advertising from anyone who didn't pay on time. She did such a good job running the paper that Benjamin Franklin wrote about her in his autobiography, saying:

> *She continu'd to account with the greatest Regularity and Exactitude every Quarter afterwards; and manag'd the Business with such Success that she not only brought up reputably a Family of Children, but at the Expiration of the Term was able to purchase of me the Printing House and establish her Son in it.*

Franklin praised Elizabeth as much for her ability as a mother as for her business skills. But she was, indeed, an excellent businesswoman and journalist.

Ann Donovan became part of the Timothy family when she married Peter Timothy in 1745. For thirty-six years, while Peter ran the paper, Ann attended to her household and raised her children. The family eventually moved to South Carolina, where Peter Timothy continued as a publisher. In 1782, Peter died in a shipwreck, and Ann Donovan Timothy followed in her mother-in-law's footsteps. She took her husband's place as printer/publisher of the paper and did such a good job that she was eventually named official printer to the state of South Carolina. Ann published the paper until her death in 1792. She left the paper to her son, Benjamin Franklin Timothy, who continued publication until he retired in 1802. The *Gazette*, South Carolina's first newspaper, provided news for the people of Charleston for nearly seventy years. If it were not for Elizabeth and Ann, this would not have been possible. In 1975, the South Carolina chapter of

Women in Communications placed a plaque at Charles Towne Landing, the site of the first South Carolina Colony, in Elizabeth's honor as the first American woman publisher.

Another important woman of colonial-era publishing was Sarah Updike Goddard. Born in 1700 in a small Rhode Island town, Sarah received an unusual education for a girl of her time. Taught by a tutor in her father's home, she learned both Latin and French, along with her English and other studies. In 1735, she married Giles Goddard, a doctor. The young couple moved to New London, where Giles practiced medicine and acted as postmaster. When Giles became ill in 1755 and could no longer perform as postmaster, Sarah took over. She also made plans for her family's future by apprenticing her fifteen-year-old son William to a printer. As an apprentice, William lived with the printer and worked for him while he learned the trade. Giles Goddard died in 1757, and when William completed his apprenticeship in 1762, the family moved to Providence, Rhode Island, where Sarah purchased equipment to set up a print shop.

According to the custom of the times, women did not conduct business on their own. William was the official owner of the paper, but in fact, William, Sarah, and her daughter Mary Katherine ran the business together. They published one of the city's first newspapers, the Providence *Gazette*. William, like his father before him, was still interested in the postal system, and he eventually became postmaster of Providence. Because the *Gazette* didn't do as well as William had hoped, he left Providence for New York in 1765 in search of a more profitable business. When he left, he suspended publication of the newspaper, but his mother and sister continued to print and sell books, almanacs, pamphlets, and other materials. Sarah also acted as postmistress, taking over William's job, just as she had for her husband. Sarah and Mary printed a special edition of the *Gazette* under the name S. & W. Goddard. The special edition was to protest the British Stamp Act, a royal tax on publications and legal documents. The Goddard women resumed regular publication of the *Gazette* in 1766, and the masthead identified the publishers as Sarah Goddard and Company (the "company" was Mary).

Mary Katherine Goddard

When Sarah died in 1770, a eulogy publicly recognizing her success as a newspaperwoman was printed in a New York and a Providence paper. Part of it read:

> *. . . she discovered an extraordinary genius and taste for, and made a surprising progress in most kinds of useful and polite learning, not only in the accomplishments to which female education is usually confined but in languages, and several branches of mathematics. . . the credit of the paper (the* Gazette*) was greatly promoted by her virtue, ingenuity and abilities . . ."*

In 1773, Mary ran the Philadelphia paper and William moved to Baltimore, where he began the Maryland *Journal.* The following year, once again answering her brother's call for help, Mary sold the Philadelphia paper to run the one in Baltimore while William concentrated on designing a new postal system. The Maryland *Journal* was published under Mary's name and was the only paper in Baltimore during most of the Revolutionary War. Mary's print shop produced the first signed copies of the Declaration of Independence. One of these rare copies is displayed today at the Smithsonian Institution.

Mary Goddard was credited with being an expert typesetter, and her paper was said to be among the best newspapers of the colonies. Staunchly patriotic, Mary reported on the cruelties of British soldiers and wrote editorials urging women to raise their own wool and flax so the colonies could be less dependent on goods from Britain. After the war, Mary struck a blow for freedom of the press by successfully suing someone who had threatened her for printing an article she didn't like. After a quarrel with William, Mary left the paper and opened a book and print shop.

Besides running the paper before and during the Revolution, Mary was appointed as postmaster of Baltimore in 1775. This made her the first woman to hold a federal office. In 1784, she hired a mailman, beginning one of the first postal delivery services in the country. Mary held the position of postmaster for fourteen years before she was replaced by a man in 1789. The job required some travel, and in this era a man could travel more easily and freely than a woman. But many people thought Mary could handle the job, and more than two hundred citizens signed a petition to allow her to remain as postmaster. Unfortunately, the petition failed, and Mary lost her job. She did, however, continue to run her bookstore until she retired in 1809 or 1810. She died in 1816.

The Goddards, the Timothys, and many other brave women of colonial America helped to lay the foundations for both American journalism and for the woman's place in journalism.

Anne **Newport Royall**

1769–1854
Pioneer Woman Journalist

> *We shall advocate the liberty of press, the liberty of speech, and the liberty of conscience.*
>
> —ANNE NEWPORT ROYALL

If Anne Royall had lived in the twentieth century, she would have been considered remarkable. In the early nineteenth century, she was truly extraordinary. At a time when few women worked outside the home and fewer women traveled on their own, this lady trekked up, down, and across the country gathering material for her writing. Then, at the age of sixty-two, she began her own newspaper.

Anne was born near Baltimore, Maryland, but spent her early years in Pennsylvania. Her childhood was filled with traumatic events. Not only did her father and, later, her stepfather die, but the family's home was wiped out in an Indian attack. When she was about seventeen, Anne and her mother walked across the Allegheny Mountains. They settled in a small town in what is now West Virginia, where her mother found work as a household servant for William Royall, a wealthy Revolutionary War hero.

Because Anne was fascinated with his large library, William Royall became her tutor. Anne and William married when she was twenty-eight and William was close to fifty. Sixteen years later William Royall died. He left most of his estate to Anne, but his niece contested the will, accusing Anne of treating him "barbarously" during his last years and of forging his will. For the next ten years, Ann lived in Alabama while she fought the case in court. The case was finally settled in favor of the niece, leaving Anne, by then close to fifty-five years old, with nothing. She moved to Washington,

D.C., and applied for a pension as the widow of a Revolutionary War veteran, but again, her efforts resulted in years of court negotiations.

This was when Anne Royall began her writing career. Traveling by stagecoach, she wandered from New Orleans to Canada interviewing people and gathering material for the ten books she would write. She earned her way as she went, placing ads in newspapers for one book while compiling notes for the next. Along the way, she met many newspaper editors and gained a reputation as a writer unafraid to voice strong opinions on almost any topic. One of her favorite targets was evangelical Presbyterians, because she felt they were overly vigorous in their efforts to convert people to their faith.

Between trips, Anne returned to Washington and became a familiar, if mostly unwelcome, figure in the halls of Congress as she tried to win her widow's pension. She eventually succeeded, but not until she was almost eighty, and then it was not much of a victory. Her husband's family claimed half the pension, and by the time she paid her legal fees and debts, she ended up with ten dollars.

In 1829, while she was in Washington, certain members of a Washington Presbyterian church, upset over her writing, decided to teach Anne a lesson. They sent a group of young boys to smash the windows of her house. Then the men stood under the broken windows praying loudly for her soul. Understandably, Anne, a woman known for her venomous temper, was not too pleased with this kind of harassment. She screamed down at the men, calling one of them an "old bald-headed son of a b---h." For this, Anne was arrested and charged with being "an evil-disposed person, slanderer, and disturber of the peace," and with "being a common scold."

The trial became a media frenzy with Anne's friends standing up for her and her enemies calling for the proper punishment for the crime—being ducked in the river. The Secretary of State appeared as a witness on her behalf, as did many of her newspaper friends who supported her right to write freely.

Anne was convicted, but the judge felt ducking was too harsh a punishment for a sixty-year-old woman. Instead, he fined her ten dollars and ordered her to pay a bond of one hundred dollars to ensure that she would keep the peace for a year. Her fines were paid by two reporter friends who felt the trial had really been about freedom of the press.

After the trial, she gave up traveling, purchased an old printing press, set it up in her kitchen, and began her first newspaper, the *Paul Pry*, in which she vowed to expose political evil and religious fraud. The paper featured Anne's opinions on controversial topics and the latest gossip about Washington figures. Fulfilling her promise, she wrote stories about such things as a minor official who used a public wagon and horses to go to the theater and how the city of Washington was contributing to cholera epidemics by refusing to either improve the city's sewage system or drain a swamp that was a breeding ground for disease. But while she was quick to condemn what she saw as evil, she was just as quick to praise what she felt was good.

Dressed in her shabby clothes (the only ones she owned), she took her papers to Capitol Hill and peddled them in the halls of Congress. Those who didn't buy one often found themselves the subject of a barbed article the following week.

Paul Pry was published for five years, but never earned Anne more than a pittance. Once President Andrew Jackson met her on her way home from the market, and seeing only a scrawny chicken in her basket, invited her to the White House for a decent meal.

Hoping to change her paper's image as nothing more than a gossip sheet, she renamed it *The Huntress*. In the first issue of the new paper, she promised to continue her pursuit of corruption, but said she would also offer literary pieces, essays, and other features. She wrote less gossip, but continued to proclaim her opinions on current affairs, speaking out for justice for American Indians, freedom of speech and the press, and free public education.

She had opinions on everything. She thought Samuel Morse's telegraph invention was wonderful, she hated slavery, but she did not approve of the tactics of abolitionists. She ridiculed Amelia Bloomer's trousers for women, and though she stood up for women's rights, she was not in favor of women's suffrage. Her campaign against overeager ministers remained vigorous, but she urged greater tolerance toward Roman Catholics and other groups. Some editors praised her for her "fearlessness of spirit," and others accused her of writing nothing but "scum and political filth."

For the fourteen years she published *The Huntress*, her paper was printed in her kitchen on a second-hand press with type that had been discarded by other printers. Because her house was often unheated in the winter, she had problems with frozen ink and paper. In the last issue of *The Huntress*, printed a few months before her death, she wrote that she had only thirty-one cents to her name and would, for the first time ever, be unable to pay her rent of six dollars. Sixty years after her burial in a pauper's grave in the Congressional Cemetery, a marker reading, "Anne Royall, Pioneer Woman Publicist," was placed at the site.

Though Anne Royall was undoubtedly an eccentric, her contributions to women and journalism were many. She was one of America's first roving correspondents and the first woman to gain a national reputation as a writer. Her boldness in standing up for the right to print what she thought advanced freedom of the press. And her diligent reporting of graft and wrongdoing in government laid the groundwork for future investigative reporting.

Sarah Josepha **Buell Hale**

1788–1879
Editor and Author

My object was . . . to illustrate the great truth that woman's mission is to educate . . . humanity.

—SARAH JOSEPHA BUELL HALE

Every child in America knows the poem "Mary Had a Little Lamb," but few people know that the author of this poem was Sarah Josepha Hale. Nor do they know that she was the person most responsible for making Thanksgiving a national holiday. But these were among the least of Sarah Hale's accomplishments.

Sarah was born on a farm in rural New Hampshire, the daughter of a Revolutionary War soldier. Like many girls of that time, she never attended school. But Sarah received an excellent education through studies with her mother and brother, who was a student at Dartmouth College. At eighteen, Sarah began teaching in the local grade school, a position she kept until she married David Hale in 1813. Nine years later she was a widow with five small children—the last one born two weeks after her husband's death. She was thirty-four years old and had no income. She opened a millinery (hat) shop, considered one of the few respectable professions for a woman, but the shop did not do well.

When she was younger, Sarah had published some articles and poems in local papers, so when her business was failing, she decided to try writing as a way to provide for her family. Her first book, a volume of poetry, was published in 1823, and a few years later her novel *Northwood: A Tale of New England* became the first successful novel written by an American woman. This success led to an offer to edit a new publication starting in Boston.

Sarah moved to Boston where she launched *Ladies' Magazine,* the first magazine for women edited by a woman. She wrote nearly the entire first edition herself. She even wrote the "Letters to the Editor" and their answers. In addition to editing the women's magazine, she also edited a children's magazine for the same publisher.

Aside from her editing job and raising her family, Sarah Hale founded the Seaman's Aid Society of Boston to help families of sailors who sometimes spent years at sea. Through this society, she helped to establish nursery schools for children and trade schools for women.

But Sarah was just getting started. In 1837, *Ladies' Magazine* was purchased by Louis A. Godey, who moved the operation to Philadelphia and changed its name to *Godey's Lady's Book.* Sarah agreed to continue as editor only if she could remain in Boston until her youngest son completed school. So, for the first few years, she edited the magazine from Boston. After her son graduated from Harvard College, Sarah moved to Philadelphia, where she edited *Godey's* until she retired at eighty-nine years old.

Mr. Godey insisted that nothing controversial be covered in his magazine, so the women who read *Godey's* read nothing about politics, religion, or economics. Even the Civil War was ignored in the pages of *Godey's*. In spite of this (or perhaps because of it), *Godey's Lady's Book* became the most popular women's magazine in the country and was considered the bible of good taste in literature, fashion, and manners. Women looked to *Godey's* not only for its elegant colored fashion plates, but for instruction on how a

Vol. CXXIII.   No. 733.

GODEY'S LADY'S BOOK.

PHILADELPHIA, JULY, 1891.

Dorothy Winstowe's Mission.

BY OLIVIA LOVELL WILSON.

Author of "O. K.," "A Knight of the Garter," etc.

WITH

ORIGINAL ILLUSTRATIONS

BY J. WILCOX SMITH.

II.

HEN with mischief and perplexity playing an active part in her precocious brain, Dorothy rushed to the garden with her beloved Giggs, revolving carefully all she had heard. Rattle-pated Dolly certainly was, but she was not dull, and what had been said of her guardian puzzled her not a little. Just how much or how little she wanted to meddle in this affair did not present itself to her, and after an unusually thoughtful half-hour, she rather pensively dragged Giggs by the collar to the house, to encounter there a surprise that filled her with delight.

Rose told her to prepare for a ride with John Neill, and be the bearer of a message from her, that she would be unable to accompany him, but sent a worthy substitute. Dorothy never doubted the latter clause. In great glee she hurried her maid as she was clad in the blue habit, and donned the gaily plumed hat, and hastened to meet John, drawing on her little gauntleted gloves.

John Neill was in the hall, waiting impatiently for Rosamond. Once more Rose had misunderstood him. Must the story of his love for her, even at this late date, be told with that humiliating confession of his unfaith to his best friend? John Neill hoped to be spared this. He had exalted ideas of honor little recognized in this century, and he could not overcome the sense of shame that filled him yet, when he remembered he had broken the tenth commandment toward the man whom he honored above all others. Still, if this knowledge *could* make Rosamond believe his love, he must even make it. Women require curious sacrifices. Yet John hardly dared hope that Rosamond loved him.

As he stood tapping his whip against his foot, he noticed Eckert Slocum lounging in an obscure window seat, and bobbing back and forth before an open window appeared Millard Thomson's head, the rest of his person being comfortably ensconced in the hammock swung on the porch.

7

The front page of an 1891 edition of Godey's Lady's Book

"proper" Victorian lady conducted herself in and out of the home. Sarah didn't hesitate to tell her readers how to behave—but always in gentle, subtle ways that would not offend even the most conservative of her "gentle readers" (or their husbands).

Sarah's advice covered every area of a woman's life. She was Heloise, Miss Manners, Betty Crocker, and Dear Abby all rolled into one. But her monthly editorials were not solely concerned with manners and home advice. Sarah continually nudged women to seek better education and wider career options, such as bookkeeping and waitressing (professions held mostly by men at that time). She believed that women were morally superior to men, but that men were stronger and better able to lead. According to this view, political concerns were inappropriate for women.

Part of Sarah's work in shaping women's attitudes toward themselves shows in her use of words. She introduced the term "domestic science" to make housekeeping seem more important. "Lingerie" was first used in the pages of *Godey's* to take the place of "underwear," which was considered to be more vulgar.

Sarah Hale's strong belief in university education for women influenced Matthew Vassar to open the country's first women's college. Sarah was gratified when Vassar opened, but she was not happy with its name— Vassar Female College. She told Mr. Vassar that the word "female" was more fit to describe animals than women. Mr. Vassar then removed "female" from the college entrance, so that it read only Vassar College.

Sarah also promoted physical fitness and exercise for women, and she discouraged certain accepted customs of the time, such as wearing overly tight corsets and sleeping in rooms with closed windows (many people believed that night air was unhealthy).

When she lived in Boston, Sarah had rented rooms in the same boarding house as Oliver Wendell Holmes, a well-known physician and writer (and the father of future Supreme Court Justice Oliver Wendell Holmes). Through him, Sarah met many writers whose stories she later published in *Godey's*, including Edgar Allan Poe, Washington Irving, Henry Wadsworth

Longfellow, and Harriet Beecher Stowe.

One of Sarah Hale's aims was to promote pride in being American. She did this in the magazine by seeking American authors, particularly women. Beyond her work on *Godey's*, she helped to raise money for a Bunker Hill monument to remember the Revolutionary War in Boston and for a restoration of Mount Vernon in Virginia as a memorial to George Washington. In her continuing zeal to promote Americanism, Sarah led a vigorous, twenty-year campaign of lobbying Congress and presidents to make Thanksgiving a national holiday. Abraham Lincoln finally proclaimed the last Thursday in November as Thanksgiving Day in 1863.

Under Sarah Hale's direction, *Godey's*, which had more than 150,000 subscribers, helped set the standards for the many women's magazines that followed. Sarah's name was known in households across the nation, both as editor of the magazine and as author of her many books for both adults and children. Many of her songs and poems were immortalized in the *McGuffey's Readers* that were used in every schoolroom in America and memorized by generations of children. Her list of published books takes up two pages, but of all her works, the one she considered most important was her 900-page anthology of biographical sketches of women, beginning with Eve and ending with women of her own time (the quote used to introduce this chapter was part of her introduction to that book).

Susan Anthony, Amelia Bloomer, and other women made fiery speeches and wrote impassioned articles on women's rights, but Sarah Hale, as editor of *Godey's Lady's Book*, did as much or more to help change the attitudes and values of nineteenth-century women. While many of her beliefs seem out of date today, she helped women overcome some of the restrictions Victorian society imposed on them in the mid-1800s. Ida Tarbell, writing about Hale much later, said she was a woman who did not fight, but one who was influential in more indirect ways.

Margaret **Fuller Ossoli**

1810–1850
Journalist, Reformer, Literary Critic

I knew that the only object in life was to grow. . . . I am determined on distinction.

—MARGARET FULLER OSSOLI

Margaret Fuller, literary critic and author of one of the first American feminist books, was as unlikely a person to be part of a revolutionary coup as one could imagine. Most of her life had been devoted to purely intellectual pursuits and to raising the educational level of women. Yet during the summer of 1849 in Italy, Margaret Fuller stood on the hills of Rome amid exploding artillery shells and detonating grenades as French forces wrested the city from the hands of Italian rebels. What was this refined, intellectual woman from Boston doing in the midst of a bloody European revolution?

Margaret was born in Cambridgeport, Massachusetts, a suburb of Boston. Her father, who desperately wanted a son as his firstborn, gave Margaret, his eldest child, the education that a son would have received. Mostly she was tutored by her father, but she did attend a private school for a year or two. Her childhood was spent in rigorous study with little time to play.

By age seven, Margaret was reading Latin, and by sixteen, Greek. In her twenties, she translated into English a volume by the German author Goethe. Later in life, Margaret wrote that she developed terrible, chronic headaches from this rigorous life of reading and study. She called her headaches her "black jailer" and the "vulture with the iron talons."

When Margaret was twenty-five, her father died, and she took a teaching position at a private school to support her mother and younger brothers and sisters. Though she earned one thousand dollars a year, a very high salary for a woman, she became bored with the lack of intellectual stimulation. She moved to Boston, where she met and became friends with Ralph Waldo Emerson and a group of intellectuals and philosophers known as Transcendentalists. As a member of this group, Margaret edited *The Dial*, the Transcendentalist magazine. In 1839, she began her series of "conversations"—weekly meetings where women met to read and discuss literature and classical philosophy. Margaret also used the groups as a forum to urge women to move beyond their traditional roles as wives and mothers. She pushed them to develop their capabilities as fully as they could in whatever direction they desired. "Let them be sea captains, if they will," she said. The meetings became so popular that Margaret eventually allowed men to attend.

In *The Dial*, Margaret wrote a series of editorials based on these forums, and out of these editorials came the material for her book *Woman in the Nineteenth Century*. This book became the basis of what would become the first strong women's movement in America. It helped set the stage for the struggle for women's suffrage. But as successful and influential as Margaret had become, her "conversations" and her editorship of *The Dial* were unpaid, volunteer positions, and she eventually ran out of money.

Horace Greeley, publisher of the New York *Tribune*, had read Margaret's work and was impressed. He offered her a job as a reporter and literary critic, which she accepted. Margaret moved to New York, where she lived with Greeley and his wife. Because it would have been unfitting for Margaret, as the only woman, to work in the *Tribune* office, she wrote from Greeley's home.

Margaret's literary criticism was well respected, and her thoughtful editorials on social problems (such as the conditions in insane asylums or women's prisons) were forerunners of what would become known as investigative journalism. But as with teaching, Margaret was not truly cut out to be a newspaper writer. Her intellect and ambition pushed her to other pursuits. "I now know all the people worth knowing in America and I find no intellect comparable to my own," she said. This was a prideful boast, but she may not have been far from wrong.

Fulfilling a wish she had had since before her father died, Margaret traveled to Europe to research the life of Goethe for a biography she wanted to write. But she did not give up her position on the *Tribune.* Horace Greeley hired her as the paper's first woman foreign correspondent, and as she toured Great Britain and France, she sent home stories about life in London and Paris.

While in England, she met Giuseppe Mazzini, the leader of the Italian Revolution who was living in exile in England. Margaret later traveled to Rome, where she met and fell in love with Giovanni d'Ossoli, the son of a nobleman and an ardent supporter of Mazzini. About a year later, she had a son by Ossoli, and they were secretly married. They left the baby with a nurse in an outlying town and returned to Rome, which was under siege by French forces. During daylight hours, Margaret dodged bullets while taking notes for her *Tribune* stories. In the evenings, after the shelling had ceased for the night, she supervised a military hospital and helped care for the wounded.

When the revolt ended in defeat for the Italian rebels, Margaret, Ossoli, and their son fled to Florence, Italy. There, Margaret became friendly with the famous poets Elizabeth and Robert Browning. Margaret's diary entries tell of much unhappiness during this period of her life. She was troubled by the scandal caused by her affair with Ossoli and the fact that their child was born before they were married. Since Ossoli was now an outcast in his own country, they borrowed enough money to return the United States. Around that time, Margaret wrote in her diary, "I am absurdly fearful, and various omens have combined to give me a dark feeling." Her words would prove to be prophetic.

The voyage across the Atlantic Ocean was an eventful one from the start. The captain of the ship died of smallpox, and Margaret's young son became ill with the same disease, but he did recover. Then, when the ship was nearly at its destination, it became stuck on a sandbar near Fire Island, New York. The ship sank after being battered by heavy waves for twelve hours. The disaster took the lives of Margaret and her family. One survivor of the tragedy recalled seeing Margaret dressed in a white night-gown, clinging to the mast of the ship, and refusing to be rescued without her child. The bodies of Margaret and Ossoli were never found, but their son's body was recovered. He is buried in Cambridge, Massachusetts, where a monument reads:

Margaret Fuller
In Riper Years
Teacher, Writer, Critic of Literature, and Art
In Maturer Age
Companion and Helper of Many
Earnest Reformer in America and Europe

All of Margaret's papers, including a manuscript she had written about the Italian revolution, were lost in the shipwreck. Horace Greeley called her "the most remarkable and in some respects the greatest woman whom America has yet known."

Sara **Payson Willis Parton**
(Fanny Fern)

1811–1872
Columnist, Author

*W*rite! Write! It will be a safe outlet for thoughts and feelings that maybe the nearest friend has never dreamed had place in your heart or brain.

— FANNY FERN

Sara Payson Willis came from a literary family. Her father founded a children's magazine and two of her brothers were successful editors. But when she began her own writing career, her brother refused to help her, saying, "I am sorry that any editor knows that a sister of mine wrote (what) you sent me." In spite of this rejection, Sara went on to become a best-selling novelist and the highest-paid newspaper columnist in the country. She was also one of the first women to have a regular column of her own.

Sara was born in Maine, grew up in Boston, and was educated at various girls' academies. She wrote for her father's paper after her graduation, but when she married Charles Eldredge in 1837, she fully intended to devote herself to marriage and children. The years 1844 to 1846 brought a series of tragedies. First her mother, then her young daughter, and finally her husband died. Her husband's death left her without support for her children, so in 1849 she married again. Her second marriage was not a good one and ended in divorce after three years. Once again on her own, Sara tried to earn money by sewing and teaching, but neither paid enough to support her children.

Turning to writing, Sara sold a couple of articles to small papers in Boston. Because they were well liked, she sought wider markets through her brother in New York. He turned her down, but his rejection only strengthened her resolve to become successful. She chose a pen name, Fanny Fern (because she remembered picking fern leaves in the spring with her mother), and continued to send her pieces to other editors, many of whom did not agree with her brother's assessment of her writing.

High school education for girls was becoming more common in the mid-nineteenth century, so more and more women were able to read. This new reading public became Fanny Fern's audience. They liked her witty, bold style, and they saw their own concerns reflected in her column. She was unafraid to discuss "forbidden" topics, such as divorce, prostitution, and even venereal disease. Part of her appeal was her use of plain, everyday words instead of the formal, flowery language used by most writers of the time. Before long, Fanny Fern's column began appearing in newspapers and magazines across the country.

In 1853, a collection of her columns was published as a book. *Fern Leaves from Fanny's Port-Folio* quickly became a best-seller. She followed this book with another, as well as one for children. In 1855, she published her first novel, the story of a woman struggling to make her own way in the world as a writer. The book caused a sensation because, unlike most novels of the day, Sara's was a realistic representation of a difficult life. The book also caused a scandal in the literary world because the story was a thinly disguised version of her own experiences and showed her brothers to be the literary snobs they were. Many considered the book shocking, but no one thought it boring. Its success led to an offer, in 1856, to write a weekly column for the New York *Ledger* for $25 a week. Sara first turned the offer down, but she changed her mind when the editor upped the price to $100.

On the day her first column appeared, she married James Parton, whom she had met when he worked for her brother's paper. In a show of support for Sara, he had quit his job when the brother refused to allow Sara's work to be printed in the paper. Sara wrote weekly for the *Ledger* until her death from cancer in 1872, never missing a column. Even after she lost the use of her right hand and had to have her head supported by a brace, she continued to write.

Along with other leading women writers of the nineteenth century, Sara Parton urged women to do and be more than just extensions of their husbands. She supported women's rights, arguing for equal pay, better job opportunities, and the vote. Her support of women extended beyond her writing, as was shown when she was elected vice president of Sorosis, the women's club she had helped found with Jane Croly.

Perhaps Sara's most important contribution to women and to journalism was her sassy, down-to-earth style, which helped make her writing easily understood by even unsophisticated readers.

The Struggle for Women's Suffrage

⇥ *The right of citizens of the United States
to vote shall not be denied or abridged by the
United States or any state on account of sex.*

— NINETEENTH AMENDMENT TO THE CONSTITUTION

⇥ *I do not wish [women] to have power over men,
but over themselves.*

— MARY WOLLSTONECRAFT, 1792

In the nineteenth century, a "proper" woman did not travel alone, and she did not make a spectacle of herself by speaking in public. Nor did she have a job. A married woman in the 1800s could not enter business contracts or control property—even if it was in her name—without her husband's approval. She could not sue for divorce unless her husband deserted her. But her husband could easily obtain a divorce, and when he did, was almost always awarded custody of the children.

The "ideal" woman of nineteenth-century America was supposed to be modest and pure, domestic and intuitive, and emotional and peaceful. Because she was considered less intelligent and physically weaker than her male counterpart, she always had to have the protection of a man. During childhood, her father had almost total control over her life, and when she married, this control passed to her husband. An unmarried woman often remained under the control of her father or brother.

This "ideal" really represented only a small percentage of women—mostly white, middle- and upper-class women who had maids and servants to do the backbreaking work of maintaining their households. At the same time, poorer women toiled as domestics or in factories. And thousands of other women stood shoulder-to-shoulder with their husbands, pushing across the frontier, breaking sod, clearing land, and fending off hostile American Indians.

Nonetheless, laws and custom supported the idea of women being the "weaker sex" who needed the protection and guidance of men.

A "respectable" woman who had to earn a living found limited opportunities. She could be a nurse, a teacher, or a librarian. Beginning in the 1840s, she might find a position as a shop clerk or as a bookkeeper in an office. If she wanted to open a business, it was either a dressmaking or millinery shop. Professions were closed to her since few colleges accepted women students. One thing a "proper" lady could do was write, but only pretty little verses or travel pieces were considered appropriate. And since the only time a lady's name appeared in print was in her birth, marriage, and death notices, she wrote under a pen name.

Yet from the beginnings of this country, some women spoke out against these restrictions. In 1776, Abigail Adams cautioned her husband, John, to "remember the ladies," when he met with the other members of the Continental Congress. He told the Congress: "We are determined to foment a rebellion and will not hold ourselves bound by any laws in which we have no voice or representation."

In 1792 in England, Mary Wollstonecraft laid the foundations for the struggle for women's rights on both sides of the Atlantic when she published her book *A Vindication of the Rights of Woman.* Sarah Hale, as editor of *Godey's Lady's Book,* called for better education and greater career opportunities for women. Margaret Fuller challenged the prevailing view of women's capabilities in her book *Woman in the Nineteenth Century.*

Women's rights were not the only social issue being debated in the 1800s. Abolitionists pushed for an end to slavery; temperance societies campaigned against the evils of alcohol; and concerns about working condi-

Women of the mid-1800s were not allowed to work in many kinds of jobs. Many women, such as these, worked as dressmakers.

tions in factories led to calls for labor reform. Actually, it was the abolition movement that first inspired large numbers of women to speak out for social change. Jane Swisshelm's abolition newspaper, the Pittsburgh *Saturday Visiter* (sic), was one of the first newspapers written and edited by a woman. Other women, such as Lucretia Mott and Sojourner Truth, broke the taboos against women speaking in public by calling for an end to slavery. These women became role models for other women who followed their lead, both by writing and by leaving their parlors and kitchens to join the men at lectures and speeches.

The historic Seneca Falls women's-rights convention of 1848

Elizabeth Cady Stanton and Lucretia Mott met for the first time at the 1840 World Anti-Slavery Convention in London. When they discovered women were not allowed to participate in the proceedings, they vowed to organize their own women's group in the United States. It took them eight years, but in 1848, Stanton and Mott headed a women's convention in Seneca Falls, New York. Susan B. Anthony and Amelia Bloomer were among those in attendance.

What had started as a meeting to promote abolition turned into a call for women's rights when Stanton read her "Declaration of Sentiments and

Resolution." Her document, patterned after the Declaration of Independence, emphasized that women had the same "inalienable" rights as men to freedom and liberty. After the meeting, Amelia Bloomer established *The Lily*, the first paper written *for* and *by* women. It quickly became a forum for women's rights and women's suffrage (the right to vote). Other women's conventions followed, along with publications advocating women's right to vote and women's rights in general.

Not all American women supported the idea of suffrage, however. Some women, remaining true to nineteenth-century ideals, felt politics and government were best left to men. Others, like Jane Swisshelm who added a plea for the right of married women to control their own property to her pleas for abolition, were more concerned with property rights and working conditions. Swisshelm believed that demanding suffrage was asking society to change too much and too quickly.

When the Civil War broke out in 1861, those women campaigning for women's suffrage turned their energies to the more immediate struggle to end slavery, hoping they would win the right to vote along with the freed slaves. But they did not. After the war, the Fourteenth Amendment was passed in 1868, granting citizenship to former slaves; the Fifteenth Amendment (1870) guaranteed former slaves' voting rights, but made no mention of gender. Women, both black and white, were excluded.

In 1869, Stanton and Anthony resumed their fight for women by forming the National Woman Suffrage Association. They called for an aggressive push for women's suffrage and full economic and political equality. The motto of their newspaper, *The Revolution*, was "Men Their Rights and Nothing More—Women Their Rights and Nothing Less."

The same year, Lucy Stone and her husband, Henry Blackwell, organized the more conservative American Woman Suffrage Association focusing only on the vote.

In 1869, women won the right to vote in Wyoming Territory. Over the next decade, some other states followed Wyoming's lead, but many did not. Still, more women were speaking out and taking an active part in politics.

In 1871, Victoria Woodhull started her own political party and ran for president.

Susan B. Anthony first called for a women's suffrage amendment to the Constitution in 1869, and in 1878, she convinced a senator from California to introduce the "Anthony Amendment," which read: "The right of citizens of the United States to vote shall not be denied or abridged by the United States or by any state on account of sex."

In 1890, the two suffrage organizations merged to form the National American Woman Suffrage Association, which was headed by younger women far more militant than Anthony and Stanton. The thrust of the new organization's arguments echoed those of Sarah Hale—that only women could influence governments to make the world more humane. But Hale believed this input should come through women's influence on men (the woman behind the man). The new belief was that this lofty goal could be achieved only through the political power of the vote—in which women had a direct impact on government.

The explosion of industrialism in the early years of the twentieth century was accompanied by more women working outside the home and by many women taking part in public affairs. No longer were women afraid to speak out, and no longer were they lulled into accepting themselves as the weaker sex. Younger leaders of the women's movement grew in prominence, including Carrie Chapman Catt, Jane Addams, and—as the voice of black women—Ida B. Wells-Barnett. The new and younger activists were far more aggressive in their approach than the previous generation. The younger leaders not only lectured, they organized and led demonstrations, marches, and protests. They chained themselves to fences. They were carted off to jail and went on hunger strikes. These stories were front-page news, and it was often women journalists who wrote them.

When the United States entered World War I in 1917, thousands of men went off to war, and women took their places in factories and offices. They worked for their country and for the war effort, yet still they could not vote. As the war drew to a close, hundreds of women marched in front of

Susan B. Anthony

A suffragist posing in front of the White House during the massive women's protest of 1917

the White House on the eve of Woodrow Wilson's inauguration, hoping to get him to support their bid for suffrage.

After years of campaigning, women were finally triumphant in 1920. Susan Anthony's amendment finally passed both the Senate and House of Representatives, and the Nineteenth Amendment became law. At last, women could voice their opinions through the ballot box in every state of the union.

Though gaining the vote was a huge victory, women were still a long way from the equality they sought. Many professions and jobs remained closed to them. Their salaries were substantially lower than their male coworkers for the same work. Women found it impossible to obtain credit in their own names. And perhaps, most of all, society still regarded women as somewhat weaker and less capable than men. Though some progress had been made, and some continued to be made through the middle years of the twentieth century, it would not be until the 1960s that the next big thrust in the struggle for women to reach equality with men would come.

Important Dates in the Struggle for Women's Suffrage (1776–1920)

1776   Abigail Adams asks that women be remembered in the Constitution.

1792   Mary Wollstonecraft, in England, writes *A Vindication of the Rights of Woman.*

1845   Margaret Fuller writes *Woman in the Nineteenth Century.*

1848   Elizabeth Cady Stanton reads her Resolutions at the first Women's Convention in Seneca Falls, New York.

1849   Amelia Bloomer publishes the first paper for and by women discussing women's rights issues.

With the passage of the Nineteenth Amendment, women were finally allowed to vote in the United States.

1869   The National Woman Suffrage Association is formed by Elizabeth Cady Stanton and Susan B. Anthony.

The American Woman Suffrage Association is formed by Lucy Stone and Henry Blackwell.

Women win the right to vote in Wyoming Territory.

1871   Victoria Woodhull runs for president of the United States.

1878   The "Anthony Amendment" is first introduced in Congress.

1890   The National Woman Suffrage Association and the American Woman Suffrage Associations merge into National American Woman Suffrage Association.

1917   More than twenty thousand women march in New York and in Washington, D.C.

1920   Nineteenth Amendment is passed as law, giving women the right to vote.

Jane **Grey Cannon Swisshelm**

1815–1884
Reformer, Journalist, Editor

T*o live is to contend, and life is finished when contentions end.*

—JANE SWISSHELM

And contentious she was! It is said that in Jane Swisshelm's passionate zeal to end slavery, she ruined Daniel Webster's chances of becoming president of the United States and drove a prominent Minnesota politician to the madhouse. Whether she was wholly responsible for these incidents is debatable, but her fiery editorials contributed to them. During Jane Swisshelm's career of more than forty years, she established four newspapers, was the first woman to sit in the press gallery on Capitol Hill in Washington, D.C., and helped to obtain better property rights for married women.

A bright and talented child, Jane learned to read by the time she was three. She also demonstrated an early talent for painting and lacemaking.

When she was seven years old, her father died, and her crafts skills enabled her to add to the family's income by teaching lacemaking and selling painted pillows to the women of her community—Pittsburgh, Pennsylvania. As the tiny child instructed the women, she listened to their discussions of the turbulent issues of the 1920s—abolition, temperance, and women's rights. By the time Jane was fourteen, she was an activist and helped to collect signatures on abolition petitions.

Jane taught school from the age of fourteen until she was twenty-one, when she married David Swisshelm. Jane called David her "dark knight" and married him against her mother's advice. They lived with David's mother, a stern woman who controlled the family's money and tried to convince Jane, a Presbyterian, to become a Methodist. David and his mother felt that, as his wife, Jane should put her own interests aside and devote herself to him. Jane reluctantly put away her painting and her books, and opened a corset-making shop to earn money while David tried unsuccessfully to get his own business underway.

The marriage was not a happy one, but in the 1800s, it was unthinkable for a woman to seek a divorce. The young couple eventually moved to Kentucky, a slaveholding state. Living in a place where slavery was legal only strengthened Jane's beliefs about the need to end slavery. In 1839, however, Jane returned to Pennsylvania to care for her ill mother. Jane remained in Philadelphia after her mother's death, teaching at a girls' school for two years. At this time, she began using the press to speak out against slavery and for women's rights, writing under the pseudonym of Jennie Dean.

In 1842, Jane returned to David, who had given up his business venture in Kentucky and was living with his mother on their farm in Pennsylvania, which Jane later renamed "Swissvale." She continued her writing, and with David's approval, began signing her own name to her work. Jane's main concern was the right of wives to control their own property. She knew from her own experience that the laws unfairly granted a husband control over his wife's property and salary. Jane's mother had left land to

Jane, but David refused to sign a deed that would have allowed her to sell the land. In 1848, largely due to her efforts, Pennsylvania passed a law giving women the right to control their own property without the approval of their husbands.

Jane's articles appeared in several publications, including Horace Greeley's New York *Tribune* and *Godey's Lady's Book,* but mostly she wrote for two abolitionist papers in Pittsburgh. When both these papers went out of business, Jane used the money from her mother's estate to begin the Pittsburgh *Saturday Visiter.* Jane was editor, reporter, and proofreader. Abolitionist papers were common at that time, but many were short-lived and all of them were run by men. Jane's paper was the only one headed by a woman, and it was a success for several years.

In 1850, Jane wrote to Horace Greeley asking if she could be his paper's correspondent in Washington, D.C. He agreed, and Jane became the first woman to sit in the press gallery in the Capitol, despite Vice President Fillmore's warning that sitting in the press box would "be very unpleasant for a lady and would attract attention." As it turned out, she only occupied her seat for one day because she left after writing an article that caused a tremendous controversy in Washington. In her article, Jane Swisshelm accused Senator Daniel Webster of secretly fathering several mixed-race children. Though the article was based on rumors and never proven, Jane wanted to discredit Webster, who supported the Fugitive Slave Law, a law that offered rewards to anyone returning runaway slaves, even if the slaves were caught in a free state. When Webster failed to gain the presidential nomination, Jane believed his failure was partly due to her article.

Although Jane spent just one day in the Washington press box, she had set a precedent and opened the way for other women to follow. She returned once again to her unhappy marriage and the next year gave birth to a daughter. When the child was six years old, Jane left David for good and moved to Minnesota, where her sister lived. David was later granted a divorce on the grounds of desertion.

In Minnesota, Jane started her second paper, the St. Cloud *Visiter.* She was offered financial backing from a prominent local Democrat on condition that she would support James Buchanan, the Democratic candidate in the upcoming presidential election. Jane agreed, but her article of "support" was really a criticism of Democratic policies. She said that Buchanan promised "the entire subversion of Freedom and the planting of Slavery in every State and Territory." The article led to a feud between Jane and the politician, which resulted in a group of his friends wrecking Jane's printing presses and the threat of a libel suit against Jane for an article insulting the wife of one of the men. Jane was reimbursed for her press, and the libel suit was withdrawn only when she agreed to retract the insult and to never again write against the Democrats in the St. Cloud *Visiter.* But Jane Swisshelm was not through speaking her mind. The very next day, she started yet another newpaper. She called it the St. Cloud *Democrat,* and she used it to continue writing against slavery in all its forms. Some time after this, the politician had a breakdown and was committed to a mental institution.

By now, Jane had overcome an earlier reluctance to speak out in public, and she traveled the entire country making impassioned pleas for her causes. In addition to her crusades for abolition and women's rights, she argued for strong government action against American Indians after she witnessed a Sioux uprising near her home in Minnesota. When the Civil War began, she made pro-Union speeches, and in 1863, she moved back to Washington, D.C., where she worked in a clerical job for the Union army. Wanting to contribute more to the war effort, she also worked as a nurse in a Union hospital and was shocked at the terrible conditions she found there. The articles she wrote for the New York *Tribune* and her paper in Minnesota helped raise money to remedy these conditions.

After the war, Jane remained in Washington and began her fourth paper. When she encountered financial problems and was unable to afford typesetters, she taught herself and other female employees how to do the work. But labor problems were not her only woes. Twice, her office (which was also her home) was set on fire by people angered by what she wrote.

She ended her newspaper career in 1866 but continued as an activist in spite of having heart disease and other ailments. In 1872, she made a lecture tour speaking in favor of women's suffrage and was a delegate to the National Prohibition Party convention. During these years, she also wrote her autobiography—using no notes. Years earlier, she had burned her diaries because the same laws that gave a husband control over his wife's property, gave him the right to read her personal papers. She died in 1884 when she was sixty-eight.

In her era, Jane Swisshelm's writing was described as "lively." Today, we would likely call it overly emotional and highly biased, but many people agreed with her views and she was popular with her readers. Someone once wrote of her: "She was a knight crusader to whom all newspaper women should doff their hats, for she fought their battles . . . and helped to open . . . doors of the future."

Amelia **Jenks Bloomer**

1818–1894
Publisher, Editor, Reformer

We . . . hear so much that is calculated to . . . impress us with a conviction of our inferiority and helplessness, that we feel compelled to . . . stand for what we consider our just rights.

—AMELIA JENKS BLOOMER

Traditional marriage vows require a woman to promise to obey her husband. The fact that Amelia Bloomer, in the mid-nineteenth century, omitted these words from her vows tells us something about her. She was a bit of a rebel, and she was fiercely independent. In one of her editorials, she said the idea that women must obey their husbands and that men who couldn't dominate their wives were unmanly was "twaddle and nonsense."

Amelia was born near Seneca Falls, New York, a town that would eventually become a historical cornerstone for the women's rights movement. But when Amelia was growing up in the 1820s, the area was still a frontier town. She later remembered playing with American Indian children when she wasn't attending school. Amelia became a teacher at the age of seventeen, but after only one term, she took a job as a governess and tutor. When she was twenty-one, she married Dexter Bloomer, who was a lawyer, editor of a small paper in Seneca Falls, and also postmaster. Amelia, under a pen name, wrote articles on temperance and abolition for Dexter's and other papers. She also acted as deputy postmaster.

When Lucretia Mott and Susan Anthony held the first Women's Rights Convention in Seneca Falls in 1848, Amelia was there. Though she did not take an active part in the historic event, she was inspired by the women she met and the speeches she heard. Soon after the convention, Amelia and a few of her friends made plans to start their own "little temperance paper." Before the project was very far along, most of the ladies abandoned the plan because it was too much work. But Amelia and one friend forged ahead to publish their paper, called *The Lily*.

From a small room attached to the post office, Amelia acted as publisher, editor, writer, and saleswoman. She solicited submissions from other women but did most of the writing herself in the earliest editions. The first *Lily* came out in January 1849 with the motto "Devoted to the interests of women" printed on the masthead. It was to be published monthly for a price of fifty cents an issue.

Though the paper was founded as a temperance journal, Amelia soon focused on women's rights and suffrage. In her editorials, she urged women to prove they were ready to accept the responsibility of voting by demonstrating their ability to organize and work for the causes they believed in. The small paper gained attention, and soon Elizabeth Cady Stanton and Susan B. Anthony were writing articles for *The Lily*. Amelia soon teamed up with Anthony and Stanton, to travel around the country making pro-suffrage speeches.

Amelia was also famous for the "Bloomer outfit," a pair of baggy trousers gathered at the ankle and the waist and worn under a loose-fitting, knee-length skirt, which was first seen by Bloomer when Libby Miller wore it on a visit to her cousin Elizabeth Stanton in Seneca Falls. Always willing to try something new, Amelia made a similar outfit for herself. She liked it so well that she wrote about it in *The Lily*, telling her readers how much more practical and comfortable it was than conventional women's clothing. She believed the style was right for "sensible" women who no longer wanted to be cramped, squeezed, and padded by heavy whalebone corsets, layers of petticoats, and skirts that dragged in the mud.

An illustration of Amelia Bloomer in her famous "bloomers."

Thousands of women flooded *The Lily* with requests for patterns and instructions on how to make the Bloomer outfit, and many agreed that the new style was more comfortable than their usual clothing. But fashion critics didn't agree. Newspapers all over the country mocked the style as unfeminine, unbecoming, and plain ridiculous. Perhaps because of the bad press, most women soon returned to wearing their petticoats and bustles. Amelia, however, stuck to her guns and continued wearing the style for about eight years. She gave it up only when she felt her dress was distracting attention from the more important issues of suffrage and women's rights.

In 1853, the Bloomers moved to Ohio, where Amelia ran *The Lily* and worked as assistant editor for a paper run by Dexter. When Amelia's printers went on strike because she had hired a woman compositor, she trained women to do these jobs normally done by men. A few years later, the Bloomers moved to Iowa. Since this was frontier country with no facilities for printing a paper and no railroad connection for easy distribution, Amelia sold *The Lily* but continued as corresponding editor until the paper ceased publication in 1856.

Though she no longer published her own paper, Amelia remained active in the fight for women's rights until she died at age seventy-six. She was a frequent speaker at meetings, and her articles were printed in several newspapers. In 1871, she was elected president of the Iowa Woman Suffrage Association, and in 1873, she helped promote a better law for women's property rights for her state.

Amelia Bloomer's contributions to women's suffrage and journalism were vital. *The Lily* was the first paper written *for* women *by* women and was the first women's suffrage journal. And her influence even spilled over to women's clothing design. While the "Bloomers" Amelia wore in the mid-1800s would seem ridiculous today, what contemporary woman's wardrobe does not contain several pairs of pants?

Jane **Cunningham Croly**
(Jennie June)

1829–1901
Columnist

I deals are not stones in the street; they are stars in the sky. They are always beyond us . . . but we can work toward them.

—JENNIE JUNE

When Jane Cunningham was twelve years old, her family emigrated from England to the United States and settled in Poughkeepsie, New York. Jane attended a girls' academy, where she not only wrote for but also edited her school paper. At the same time, she wrote articles for local papers in her community. In 1855, she set out to seek a journalism career in New York City. Like most women writers of her day, she wrote under a pen name so as not to embarrass her family. The name she chose, Jennie June, came from a line in a poem once given to her by a family friend, who told her she was the "Juniest" Jennie he knew.

Jennie June's first newspaper column for the New York *Tribune*, called "Parlor and Side-Walk Gossip," quickly led to other assignments. She successfully convinced her editor that he could greatly increase their reader-ship by including features in his paper that appealed directly to women. She was right. New York women, who until then had not read newspapers, became avid fans, eagerly awaiting Jennie June's latest words on what fashions to wear and which to avoid. This started what grew to be an important part of practically every newspaper in the country—special women's sections and features.

Jennie June warned against silly and frivolous fashions that got in a woman's way, such as long skirts that picked up dirt from the street. She also advised against wearing the very tight corsets that were the fashion of the day because they restricted breathing. But though she advocated more sensible clothing, she joined those who criticized the "radical" styles worn by Amelia Bloomer and her friends.

Jenny June did not endorse suffrage but she was a firm believer in a woman's right to have a career outside the home. She urged her readers to break into new fields such as bookkeeping, secretarial work, and even retail store management. But while she advocated outside careers, she also told her readers that homemaking and child-raising were in themselves worthy pursuits. Although she herself did little housework, she wrote many books on housewifery skills.

Jane Cunningham married another journalist, David Croly, in 1856, and shortly after their marriage the couple moved to Illinois. They both worked as editors on the same newspaper, but Jane missed the big city, so they returned to New York a year later. Jane joined the staff of the New York *World*, where she later became editor of the women's department. David eventually left journalism and became active in philosophical and religious pursuits, leaving Jane to be the main breadwinner for the family.

Jane did this quite well. Instead of writing for only one paper at time, she arranged what she called a "duplicate system of correspondence." Basically, she sold her columns to several newspapers, making her the first syndicated columnist. Today, dozens of syndicated columnists' articles appear in daily papers across the country. Jane's system marked the beginning of an important change in journalism. Up to that time, a writer's work could be reprinted in other newspapers, but the writer received no additional payment. With syndication, the writer sold an article to several publications and was paid by each.

In addition to her newspaper columns, Jane also became the chief writer for *Demorest's Quarterly Mirror of Fashion,* and *Godey's Lady's Book,* two of the most popular women's magazines of the mid-1800s. While she was best known for women's features, she also wrote about major news events, such as the initial run of the *Silver Palace* (the first sleeper Pullman train) and the maiden voyage of the *Tokio* (the largest steamship of the day).

Jane ran her life on a strict schedule. She reserved mornings to stay at home with her five children and went to the office after lunch, often remaining there until well past midnight. Though Jane felt she had successfully combined a full-time career with motherhood, at least one of her sons did not agree. He complained that she spent too much time at work and not enough with him. It is interesting to note, though, that this son, Herbert David Croly, followed his mother into journalism and became editor of a prestigious magazine, *The New Republic.*

By the end of the 1800s, journalism was beginning to be acknowledged as a legitimate profession and courses in journalism were being offered in universities. In recognition of Jane Croly's contributions and knowledge, she was granted an honorary Ph.D. in Literature from Rutgers Women's College in 1892 and appointed as the first woman professor of journalism at the same school. (Rutgers Women's College has no relation to the modern Rutgers University.)

In spite of her heavy workload and her commitment to her children, Jane devoted a good deal of her time to the women's club movement she had helped start. She felt these clubs were important because they provided forums where women found the educational and cultural enrichment that could help lead them out of their age-old confinement to the kitchens and parlors. In 1889, Jane helped form the General Federation of Women's Clubs and that same year, began the Women's Press Club of New York.

She wrote her columns until she was forced into retirement at the age of seventy-one due to a broken hip. That same year, 1898, her 1,117-page book on the history of women's clubs in America was published. She died three years later, four days after her seventy-second birthday.

Jane Croly is best remembered with her own words, written near the end of her life, "I have never done anything that was not helpful to women, so far as lay in my power."

Miriam (Frank) Florence
Folline Leslie

1836–1914
Editor, Publisher

Known in the late 1800s as the "Empress of Journalism," Miriam Leslie owned and ran several popular magazines and newspapers. At a time when $1,000 a year was considered a good income, she was earning $100,000 a year. Miriam lived a colorful and highly unconventional life, paying little attention to the social restraints of her time. She was the subject of numerous scandals concerning her four marriages and several love affairs. Before becoming a writer and editor, she even had a brief career on stage.

Miriam was born in New Orleans and grew up in New York. She once said she had "a pinched and starved little childhood." In spite of this, she received an excellent education and was fluent in French, Spanish, and Italian, as well as English. At seventeen, she married a much older man, but she never lived with him and the marriage was later annulled. After the annulment, she tried her hand as an actress, appearing in several plays.

In 1857, Miriam married Ephraim George Squier, an entrepreneur and infrequent writer for Frank Leslie, a publisher of several successful magazines and newspapers. After her marriage, Miriam began contributing articles to Leslie's publications, and in 1863, she was named as editor of one of them—*Lady's Magazine*. The following year, she established *Frank Leslie's Chimney Corner*, which she also edited. Her next achievement was editing *Frank Leslie's Lady's Journal*, which, under her leadership became one of the country's leading fashion magazines.

In 1873, Miriam divorced her husband and the following year married Mr. Leslie. She continued editing, but only two days a week. The rest of her time was spent as a member of New York's social set, entertaining celebrities, millionaires, and world leaders. She developed expensive tastes and was once said to have worn more than $70,000 worth of diamonds.

In the late 1870s, she toured the country and wrote several books about life in the booming West. In one of these books, she criticized the immorality in Virginia City, Nevada, a rough-and-tumble mining town. In retaliation, a newspaper in that city wrote an article revealing shocking information about her personal life, probably about her affair with Leslie while she was still married to Ephraim George Squier.

By the time Frank Leslie died in 1880, his business was bankrupt, and Miriam inherited a $300,000 debt. It was at this point in her life that Miriam really showed what she could do. Determined to restore the Leslie publishing empire, she lowered her style of living and focused on rebuilding the business, writing that she now knew what it was like to live "in a carpetless [apartment]." She made a number of smart business moves, including changing her name legally to Frank Leslie and reducing the number of her publications from twelve to six. In the fifteen years she headed the company, she managed 400 employees, met a weekly payroll of $32,000 and increased her own income to $100,000.

During this same period, she remained active in New York high society,

Vol. XXV.—No. 4.   APRIL, 1888. $3.00 PER ANNUM.

FRANCE'S BULWARKS.

At the present time, when the greatest Powers of Continental Europe are vying with each other in gigantic military preparations, and when the designs of France are a theme of general interest, it will be interesting to consider her military strength, which there seems a general tendency to underestimate. It can but be evident, upon even a most casual inspection, that since her great overthrow in 1871, France has made rapid and surprising

Vol. XXV., No. 4—25.   INSIDE THE GREAT FORTRESS AT VERDUN.

The front page of an 1888 edition of **Frank Leslie's Popular Monthly**

made several trips to Europe, and carried on several romances. After one of her European trips, she began calling herself the "Baroness de Bazus," which she claimed was an ancestral title.

Miriam's writing appeared as syndicated articles for the American Press Association and in the *Ladies' Home Journal,* as well as in her many books. In 1889, she sold her weekly, *Illustrated Newspaper,* and in 1895 leased her other publications to a syndicate. But three years later, when the syndicate failed, Miriam once again took over as editor of her one remaining magazine, *Frank Leslie's Popular Monthly* and rebuilt its circulation to over 200,000. This success was short-lived, however. In 1900, Miriam sold the paper due to financial problems and gave up editing. She died in 1914 at age seventy-eight and left more than $1 million to Carrie Chapmam Catt for "the furtherance of the cause of women suffrage."

Victoria C. **Woodhull**

1838–1927
Reformer, Orator, Journalist

Victoria Woodhull's life is one of the most peculiar stories in the history of journalism. Aside from her journalism career, she was a medicine-show fortune-teller, a medium who conducted seances, a successful Wall Street stockbroker, a popular lecturer, a spokeswoman for women's rights, a radical social reformer, and a philanthropist. Her enemies accused her of being a blackmailer and swindler, while her admirers saw her as a person unafraid to speak out against hypocrisy and corruption. More than anything else, Victoria was a woman born before her time. She believed that women should vote and hold public office and that women could successfully compete against men in business. Many of her ideas, laughed at in the 1870s, are readily accepted in the late twentieth century.

Victoria Claflin was born in Homer, Ohio. Her mother was a strong believer in spiritualism, and Victoria later claimed that she, too, saw mystical visions as early as age three. She said she spoke to the spirits of her dead sisters.

While Victoria was very young, her family was chased out of town by angry citizens who suspected Mr. Claflin of setting fire to his gristmill to collect insurance. For the next several years, the Claflins sold home-bottled remedies in their traveling medicine show. Victoria and her younger sister, Tennessee, were the stars of the show. They were featured as fortune-tellers and psychic readers.

At fifteen, Victoria married Canning Woodhull. Tennessee joined her sister and Canning, and the three traveled through the Midwest with Victoria and Tennessee conducting seances. At a seance, people are supposedly put in contact with the spirits of dead relatives and friends; a medium is a person who conducts such seances and claims to have a psychic link to the afterlife.

Victoria divorced Canning after she fell in love with Colonel James Blood. Blood, an older and well-educated man, taught Victoria history and politics and helped her to polish her manners and style.

In 1868, Victoria had another vision. She said Demosthenes, the ancient Greek orator, appeared to her and told her to go to a certain address in New York, where she would find a house waiting for her. He also told her she would attain the fame and fortune for which she had yearned all her life. Of course, Victoria wasted no time getting to New York, where she did, indeed, find a house. She took not only her children from her first marriage and new husband, but her sister Tennessee, her parents, and her other siblings!

Her house in New York quickly became a gathering place for spiritualists and a group of liberal freethinkers. Shortly after they arrived in New York, the sisters met Commodore Cornelius Vanderbilt, a millionaire railroad tycoon. Vanderbilt believed in spiritualism, and when Tennessee offered to be his medium, he was delighted. Vanderbilt helped the sisters by giving them tips about investing in the stock market. He also helped them establish their own brokerage house, making the sisters the first lady brokers on Wall Street.

After Victoria conquered Wall Street, proving a woman could be successful in business, she was ready for a new challenge—politics. In 1870,

Victoria decided to run for president of the United States. This was when she began her journalism career. First, she wrote several articles for the New York *Herald* and even had her own column, "Petticoat Politician." But she needed a better way to promote her candidacy and to express her other beliefs to the public.

In May 1870, she and her sister started the *Woodhull & Claflin's Weekly.* The paper was funded by the earnings from their brokerage firm and money from Commodore Vanderbilt. Victoria was editor and publisher, and Colonel Blood and others did much of the writing. In addition to articles supporting Victoria for president, her paper contained pieces on social problems, women's careers, historical essays, a serialized novel by George Sand (a woman), theater reviews, fashion, financial columns, sports, and advertisements. There were also articles about spiritualism and other topics that were very controversial. One of Victoria's main thrusts was women's suffrage. The Fourteenth and Fifteenth Amendments to the Constitution, passed shortly after the end of the Civil War, gave full citizenship and the vote to former slaves. Victoria argued that these amendments should include women.

In 1871, Victoria arranged a hearing before the House of Representatives where she made an appeal for women's suffrage. The date of Victoria's speech was January 11, the same day the National Woman Suffrage Association's third annual convention was being held in Washington, D.C. This was no accident. Victoria had planned it that way. Susan B. Anthony, Elizabeth Cady Stanton, and several other suffrage ladies attended Victoria's speech and were surprised to find her intelligent and compelling. Stanton invited Victoria to address the suffrage convention that evening. Victoria began her speech with these inspiring words: "We mean treason; we mean secession. . . .We are plotting revolution!" The convention responded with enthusiastic cheers.

For most of the next year, Colonel Blood and her sister ran the paper while Victoria traveled the country lecturing on women's rights and other topics. At first, Stanton and Anthony supported her, but at the next suf-

Victoria Woodhull addresses a congressional committee on the issue of women's suffrage.

frage convention, Victoria suggested that the women start their own political party and nominate her for president. Susan Anthony felt Victoria was trying to take over the organization and refused Victoria permission to address the meeting. Did Victoria run away and hide? Absolutely not. She held her own convention and started the Equal Rights Party, which nominated her as its presidential candidate. And Frederick Douglass, the highly respected African-American speaker and diplomat was named as her running mate. Douglass, who was not present at the nomination, later declined the offer.

Then Victoria did something that would have far-reaching results. In November 1872, shortly before the election, she printed a story in the *Weekly* about an affair between the prominent clergyman Henry Ward Beecher and the wife of another man. The public was outraged! People did not want to believe the things Victoria was saying about Beecher, even if they were true. But at the same time, many people loved reading all about the juicy details of the affair. The Beecher story became the scandal of the century. The paper sold out so quickly that people were selling their own copies for as much as forty dollars each.

Victoria was arrested and put on trial for printing "obscene" material. Though she was eventually acquitted, she was in jail on Election Day. As it turned out, she received very few votes, and her run for the presidency simply collapsed. After the election, she was released on bail and restarted regular publication of the *Weekly*. She wrote about how unfairly she had been treated and about the hypocrisy of people like Beecher. The paper enjoyed renewed popularity, but only for a while. Over the next few years, the paper was printed irregularly, and the last issue was in June 1876. By now Victoria and Blood were divorced, and Victoria had lost both her mansion and the stock-brokerage business.

Her life took a surprising turn when her old friend Commodore Vanderbilt died. Though neither Victoria nor Tennessee were mentioned in his will, they did receive a large sum of money from his estate. Victoria and Tennessee then moved to England. Victoria started a new paper, the *Humanitarian*, with her daughter as associate editor. She also met and eventually married John Biddulph Martin, a wealthy English banker. Tennessee also married in England and became a baroness.

As Mrs. Martin, Victoria once again had a great deal of money. Throughout her later years, she wrote about women's rights, social causes, and educational reform. When she died at eighty-eight years old, she left a large endowment for a women's agricultural college.

Even today, many people see Victoria Woodhull as an eccentric radical, but her contributions to women and journalism are valid. Her reports exposing corruption, injustice, and hypocrisy helped lay the groundwork for social changes that eventually took place. It was her initiative in proclaiming herself as a presidential candidate that spurred the women's suffrage movement into aggressive action. But above all else, Victoria Claflin Woodhull stands out as an example of a person unafraid to speak out for what she believed even when she knew it was unpopular.

Kate **Field**

1838–1896
Journalist, Author, Lecturer, Actress

I should be perfectly miserable if I thought that I could never write. . . . I prefer the fame of an author.

—KATE FIELD, WRITING IN HER CHILDHOOD DIARY

Kate Field was born in St. Louis, Missouri. Her father was a newspaper publisher and her mother an actress. Kate's parents indulged her with a personal maid and French and music lessons. As young as age three, she was reciting lines from Shakespeare's *Hamlet.* At eight, she wrote her first story, which was published in her father's paper.

Kate left home when she was sixteen to attend an exclusive girls' school in Boston, where she lived with an aunt and uncle. Shortly before she graduated, Kate's father died. He left no estate. Young Kate was rescued from poverty by her aunt and uncle, who supported her financially and treated her like their own daughter. Kate was grateful, but she yearned for independence. Shortly before leaving for a European tour in 1859 with her aunt and uncle, she arranged with the editor of a Boston paper to send him articles about her travels. She was to be paid five dollars for each one he used.

In Europe, Kate met leading literary figures such as Elizabeth and Robert Browning and George Eliot. The articles she sent home were filled with lively and entertaining tidbits about her new friends and others in high society. However, to the surprise of her editor, she also wrote some serious pieces. Kate's writing later reflected that up to this period in her life, she had not thought deeply about anything—most of her ideas were those she had inherited from her uncle. But her association with writers and intellectuals caused her to think for herself, and she discovered she had ideas unlike her uncle's. She realized that one point on which she strongly disagreed with her uncle was slavery. He was in favor of it, but Kate was not, and she wrote articles favoring abolition.

When her uncle read her anti-slavery writings, he was furious and threatened to withdraw his financial support and to disinherit her unless she stopped. But Kate followed her own conscience. Vowing to support herself, she returned to the United States in 1861. In a move to establish herself as a serious journalist, she joined forces with Jane Croly and helped found Sorosis, the first important women's club, and the first women's newspaper club.

In the mid-1800s, many people were fascinated with spiritualism. Ouija boards became popular, as did seances and other attempts to communicate with the world beyond. Kate, always one to keep up with the latest fad, wrote a book about her experiences of being guided by the planchette, an oval glass ball that moves over the ouija board answering "yes" or "no" to questions.

As Kate became more well known, she traveled the country giving lectures. She loved to perform and now she had the chance. Some of her lectures were speeches on various topics, but others were one-woman shows featuring dramatic readings from Charles Dickens's writings or her song-and-dance routine making fun of English aristocracy. She became so popular that she earned eight thousand dollars a year from her appearances. In

1874, she entered the world of serious acting when she debuted as a Broadway actress.

In 1890, Kate followed in Anne Royall's footsteps by moving to Washington, D.C., and starting her own newspaper, *Kate Field's Washington*. The paper was written almost entirely by Kate and was filled with her opinions on current topics. She urged the government to purchase John Brown's farm in New York and make it into a national monument. John Brown, a white man who led an unsuccessful slave rebellion, was considered a terrorist by some and a hero by others. Kate also wrote articles supporting statehood for Alaska and Hawaii; prodding Congress to reform marriage laws; and advocating better copyright laws to protect writers. And while in her younger years, she had not been a supporter of women's suffrage, Kate did come out for it in her own paper.

By 1896, Kate Field had a new interest and stopped writing her paper. She left Washington to join a cruise headed first to Hawaii, then to Japan to witness a solar eclipse. Unfortunately, she fell off a horse during the stopover in Hawaii and contracted pneumonia while she was recovering. Though she was ill, she insisted on taking the cruise to Japan, but died before the day of the eclipse. She was fifty-seven years old. Today, Kate Field's name is not much more than a footnote in journalism history, but she should be remembered as a trailblazer, one of the first women to achieve independence, fame, and success in several different fields.

Eliza Jane **Poitevent Holbrook Nicholson**

1849–1896
Publisher, Poet

Nobody knows what a woman can do, least of all the woman herself, until she tries.
—ELIZA JANE NICHOLSON

Eliza Jane Poitevent grew up on the Louisiana-Mississippi border, where she was raised to become a true Southern belle who would spend her time sipping mint tea at garden parties. But Eliza Jane was an independent young woman who had different ideas for herself. And though she remained in all respects the well-bred Southern gentlewoman she was raised to be, she defied tradition many times. First, she went to work on a city newspaper. Then she married her boss, a divorced man forty years older than herself. And when her husband died she took over as publisher of the New Orleans *Picayune,* making her the first woman to head a major newspaper in the South.

As a young child, Eliza had few playmates except for the birds and small animals of the woods and meadows near her home. Perhaps because she spent so much of her time alone, she began writing poetry, often with her pet canary perched on her finger. Using the pen name Pearl Rivers, after the waterway that ran alongside her home, she submitted her work to literary journals while still in her teens. She attended and graduated from a local finishing school but later said she had "learned nothing that was of much use to me."

When Eliza was twenty, she met Alva Holbrook while visiting her grandfather in New Orleans. Holbrook, the owner and editor of the New Orleans *Picayune,* offered her a job as literary editor on his paper for twenty-five dollars a week. Eliza didn't listen to her family, who told her going to work, particularly at a city newspaper, was unladylike. She accepted the job and became the first woman on the staff. Working for the *Picayune,* she helped to introduce readers to the best literature in the United States by featuring stories by Mark Twain, Joel Chandler Harris, and Bret Harte.

Two years later, she married the sixty-five-year-old Holbrook. Her family objected to the match, more because the man had been divorced than because of his age. During her marriage to Holbrook, Eliza spent less time working at the paper and more time working on her own poetry, publishing a book of her poems in 1873. In 1876, Holbrook died, and Eliza inherited the newspaper, along with its debt of more than eighty thousand dollars.

Once again, she scorned the advice of her family and decided not to sell the troubled paper, but to run it herself. She knew that working for a woman might be an unsettling experience for her male staff members. She told the staff that she promised no hard feelings to any who wished to leave, and she asked those who stayed to pledge their loyalty to reestablishing the success of the paper. Relying on her own exceptional intelligence and intuition, plus help on the business end from George Nicholson, a staff member and stockholder, Eliza brought new life to the *Picayune.* Under her leadership, the paper doubled in size and increased its circulation from six thousand to twenty thousand.

Eliza could not have succeeded in running a major newspaper without a good deal of courage and strength. But at the same time, Eliza was truly a shy woman who never really had confidence in her own abilities. Shortly after taking over the *Picayune*, she said:

> *I never felt so lonely and little and weak in my life as on the first day when I took my seat in Mr. Holbrook's big editorial chair, and for months afterward my lack of confidence was so great that I used to wonder why the staid old* Picayune, *accustomed to being managed by such wise old fellows . . . didn't just roll over and split its sides laughing at me.*

In 1878, Eliza and Nicholson were married, and they continued running the paper together—she was the editor, and he was the business manager. After the birth of their two sons (in 1881 and 1883), Eliza divided her time between her family and the paper, and also found time to write more poetry.

As owner of the *Picayune*, Eliza used her influence to force the city into improving the water system, as well as the police and fire departments. Putting her love of animals into action, she formed the Louisiana Band of Mercy, a children's group dedicated to protecting animals. This group later grew into the Louisiana branch of the Society of Prevention and Cruelty to Animals. Because she felt the education most young ladies received at that time produced "the most helpless and most pathetic class of people in the world . . . who are thrown on their own resources without one solitary qualification," she promoted a free night school that offered practical courses.

Eliza's contributions to journalism were many. Her paper was the first in the South and one of the first in the country to offer special sections for women and children. She encouraged other women to enter newspaper work and hired one as her Washington correspondent. She launched the career of Dorothy Dix, who became the nation's most famous advice columnist. Among the many features she brought to the *Picayune*, were medical advice columns, illustrations, sports coverage, and comic strips.

One of her most popular innovations was the weather frog, a cartoon weather forecast. The society column she introduced, a first for New Orleans, initially displeased the city's elite, but later became a favorite feature. She also added a section she called "The Picayune Telephone," where readers could air complaints about local businesses and government, a feature still popular in many local papers.

In 1896, both Eliza and her husband died during an influenza epidemic. She was just forty-six years old. There is no way to tell what great accomplishments she might have made if her life had not been cut short.

Gertrude **Bustill Mossell**
(N. F. Mossell)

1855–1948
Journalist, Feminist, Educator

It was not surprising that Gertrude Bustill Mossell became one of the most accomplished African-American women in the nineteenth century. She was carrying on a long family tradition of political and civil activism. Her great-grandfather was Cyrus Bustill, a freed slave who was a baker for George Washington during the Revolutionary War and later became a teacher. Two of her cousins, Grace Bustill Douglass and Sarah Mapps Douglass were well-known abolitionists. Another cousin, Paul Robeson, a famous actor and political activist, was one of the few African-American men ever to win a coveted Rhodes scholarship. Gertrude Mossell earned her own fame as an outstanding journalist who spoke out for women's suffrage and civil rights.

Gertrude was born and grew up in Philadelphia, Pennsylvania. Because Gertrude was quite young when her mother died, she boarded with relatives until she was twelve years old, when she went to live with her father. As a young child, she read any books available to her, and when there were no more books to read, she read the encyclopedia. An excellent student, she graduated as valedictorian (a prize awarded to the student with the highest grade average) of her grammar-school class. Reverend Benjamin Tucker Tanner, editor of the *Christian Recorder,* was in the audience at the graduation ceremony and was so impressed with her speech that he published it in his paper. He also hired Gertrude as a part-time correspondent.

In the 1870s, a grammar-school diploma was about the same as today's high school diploma. And to become a teacher in the 1870s, all one needed was a grammar-school diploma. So Gertrude began two careers—one as a teacher and one as a journalist. For seven years, Gertrude taught school in Philadelphia, New Jersey, and Kentucky. During this same period of time, she wrote for three Philadelphia papers.

By the time she was twenty-five, she was editor of the women's page for two newspapers. A few years later, she was the author of her own column in the New York *Freeman*, which she said would be "devoted to the interests of women" and "promote true womanhood." Both the New York *Freeman* and its star columnist, Gertrude Mossell, went on to gain national reputations. Gertrude's column, syndicated in African-American newspapers throughout the country, consistently encouraged women to seek careers in medicine, journalism, and teaching, and to volunteer for community service.

In 1880, Gertrude married Nathan F. Mossell, a prominent physician. After her marriage, she signed her articles as N. F. Mossell. In 1894, she published *The Work of the Afro-American Woman,* a book analyzing the place of African-American women in society.

Not only did Gertrude push her readers toward greater achievement, she also prodded her colleagues in the African-American press to aim for higher professional standards by improving both the quality of their writing and by covering a wider range of topics. She also helped to increase profits of black papers by recommending hiring young newsboys to sell papers on street corners, just as white mainstream papers did. But most black papers relied only on prepaid subscriptions for sales. In one of her articles, Gertrude noted "I have never seen a colored newspaper sold on the streets by a newsboy."

Gertrude was a strong supporter of women's suffrage and of civil rights, but she refused to join white suffragist groups because she felt they discriminated against African-Americans. She also organized African-American women's groups and worked to help African-American women gain recognition for their accomplishments and abilities.

Aside from her newspaper writing, Gertrude Mossell wrote one children's novel and several poems. She helped to found the Bustill Family Association and the Philadelphia branch of the National Afro-American Council, a forerunner of the NAACP.

At a time when few women worked outside the home, Gertrude successfully combined her career with raising her two daughters, Maize and Florence. From the start of her journalism career, she called for her readers to engage in what she called "racial uplift." Gertrude Mossell's legacy most certainly contributed to that uplifting.

Ida Minerva **Tarbell**

1857–1944
Journalist, Biographer, Lecturer

A thing won by breaking the rules of the game is not worth the winning.

—IDA TARBELL

Ida Tarbell grew up in a boisterous western Pennsylvania boomtown where oil had recently been discovered. Her father was the inventor of the first wooden oil-storage tanks. He was a prosperous oil producer until John D. Rockefeller's growing industrial empire forced him out of business. At the time, no one suspected that Ida would one day write an exposé of Rockefeller's Standard Oil Company and its strong-arm business practices.

Ida's parents brought her up to be independent and to think for herself. A headstrong child, she rebelled against doing homework and sometimes skipped school, but as she matured, she became more interested in her studies. Part of her inspiration to study was her mother's suffragette friends and her family's participation in the Chautauquan society, a group that offered educational and cultural programs.

Independence and education became Ida's prime motivators. And because she believed that she'd be neither independent nor free to get an education if she were to marry, she vowed at fourteen to remain single for life. She planned to become a biologist and attended Allegheny College, where she was the only girl in the freshman class and one of only four girls in the entire school. When she graduated in 1880, nobody was willing to hire a woman biologist, so she began her career in one of the few fields open to women—teaching school. Ida found that she didn't particularly like teaching, so after two years, she became an editor and writer for the *Chautauquan* magazine, a position she held for eight years.

Tired and bored with her life, Ida decided to do something that truly inspired her. In 1891, she moved to Paris to research women who took part in the French Revolution. She focused her studies on a Madame Roland, whose biography she wanted to write. Life in Paris was a struggle for a woman with little money. Ida lived in a tiny Left Bank apartment, studying history at the Sorbonne in the mornings and researching Madame Roland in the afternoons. Though she sold occasional articles about life in Paris to American magazines, her money dwindled to almost nothing. At one point, she had to pawn her coat and watch to buy food.

Then, one day, a young man named S. S. McClure knocked on her door. He said he enjoyed her writing and wanted her to work for a new magazine he was launching. He then asked if he could borrow forty dollars. Because Ida knew how tough it was to be broke, she gave him the loan even though she could not spare the money and was sure she would never hear from him again. But McClure surprised Ida. He eventually returned her money and then convinced her to return to the United States to join his staff. His magazine, *McClure's*, quickly became one of the most popular serious magazines in the country, largely due to Ida's writing.

Ida Tarbell's first series of articles for *McClure's* was a biography of Napoleon, which was later published as a book. The following year, with McClure's help, her biography on Madame Roland was published. She followed with several studies of Abraham Lincoln, most of which appeared first as series of articles in *McClure's* and later as books.

Ida's writing was not limited to biographies. McClure wanted his writers to do articles exposing unscrupulous practices of big business, and he suggested that Ida take on Standard Oil Company as her project. Because Ida remembered her father and others like him who had lost their businesses to Rockefeller, she was enthusiastic about the project. She even proceeded after her father warned her that Rockefeller would retaliate and ruin the magazine.

President Theodore Roosevelt called this type of writing "muckraking," implying that Ida and others who wrote exposés were emphasizing everything bad and nothing good about American business. But Ida didn't think of herself as a muckraker. In fact, she helped pioneer a new type of investigative journalism. The new reporting was based not on sensationalism and hearsay, but on carefully documented research. For more than two years, Ida conducted interviews with Henry H. Rogers, vice president of Standard Oil, and she pored over reams of old company records.

Always a gentlewoman, Ida's visits with Rogers were friendly until the day she confronted him with secret information a former employee of the company had sent her. After that confrontation, she was no longer welcome at Rogers's office, yet she continued her investigation on her own. "The more intimately I went into my subject," she said, "the more hateful it became to me."

Ida never spoke to Rockefeller—he refused to see her. But to get a feel for what kind of person he was, she quietly followed him around town. She even attended his church on several Sundays to watch him. While Ida hated Rockefeller's methods, she admired his drive, his intelligence, and the vast amounts of money he donated to charities. She pointed out all of these good qualities in her writing.

Ida's series on Standard Oil ran in *McClure's* from November 1902 to April 1904. They were a colossal hit. By exposing many of the company's deceptive practices, Ida was responsible for a government investigation and the eventual enactment of anti-trust laws to prevent giant corporations from forming monopolies that wiped out competition from smaller businesses. Ida was hailed as the "Joan of Arc," of the oil industry and became one of the best-known writers in America. And her career was just getting started.

In 1906, Ida and other writers for *McClure's* left that magazine to start their own, which they called *The American Magazine*. Besides writing for the new magazine, Ida wrote biographies of other business leaders. In her later years, she was often accused of "selling out" to big business because her biographies were so complimentary. But Ida responded that she had never set out to write exposés—only to report the truth.

When *The American* was sold to a large publishing company in 1915, Ida became a lecturer for the Chautauqua Society. Like other Americans, Ida was deeply affected by World War I (1914–18). No longer did she think mainly of the United States and its citizens. Her focus shifted to the problems that faced the entire world. For the next seventeen years she lived a grueling schedule, traveling around the country speaking about international relations, social responsibility in business, and peace and disarmament. During the war, she was a member of the Women's Committee of the United States Council of National Defense and a delegate to many international and governmental conferences. She continued to work for world peace to the end of her life, but she also found time to write several more books, many of them about Abraham Lincoln.

In spite of her own independence, Ida was never a supporter of women's suffrage. In her book *The Business of Being a Woman* she wrote, "women had a business assigned by nature and society which was of more importance than public life." This seems to go against her own life choices and may reveal that she had second thoughts on her decision never to marry. Or perhaps she thought of herself as different from most other women.

Ida Tarbell remained active until late in life. In her seventies, she taught courses on writing biographies at several colleges. She was eighty-two when she wrote her autobiography, *All in a Day's Work*. She died of pneumonia at eighty-six. Ida's most important legacy to journalism was her scrupulous verification of everything she wrote, which helped to set new standards for investigative journalism. Of her many books and articles, *The History of Standard Oil Company* remains her most important and most remembered work. Today, many people call her the "grandmother of muckrakers."

Elizabeth **Meriwether Gilmer** (Dorothy Dix)

1861–1951
Crime Reporter and Advice Columnist

*R*emember that you get out of life just exactly what you put into it.

—DOROTHY DIX

Elizabeth Gilmer never intended to become one of the most famous advice columnists in America. In fact, she never even thought about working because in the late 1800s, most women of her social class did not work. But shortly after she married, Elizabeth discovered that her husband suffered from a serious mental illness. Because he was unable to work, Elizabeth had to find a way to earn a living for both of them. This was too much for the young woman to cope with. She had a nervous breakdown and was sent to Bay Saint Louis on the Mississippi Gulf Coast to recover.

Her writing career began when her neighbor, Eliza Nicholson, owner and publisher of the New Orleans *Picayune,* offered her a job. The meeting was a lucky break for both of them. Elizabeth found new meaning for her life, and Mrs. Nicholson had a talented new writer on her staff. Elizabeth's first job at the *Picayune* was writing obituaries and fillers. She studied dictionaries and books of synonyms to improve her vocabulary, and read every newspaper she could get her hands on to improve her journalistic skills.

One day Mrs. Nicholson suggested that Elizabeth write an advice column addressed to women. Following the fashion of the day, Elizabeth's first task was to choose a pen name. She chose "Dorothy" because she liked the name, and "Dix" to honor a much-loved former slave who had belonged to her family before the Civil War. Her column was called "Sunday Salad," but was soon changed to "Dorothy Dix Talks."

Most letters to Dorothy Dix's column came from young women in the throes of lost loves or in agony over which man to choose. But other letters asked truly difficult questions—often questions to which there were no good answers. Women sought advice about husbands who refused to provide enough money to run the household. Others asked for help with straying husbands, difficult in-laws, and disobedient children.

This was the height of the Victorian Age, a time when women were expected to be dependent weaklings. It was also a time when people were expected to live their lives according to strict social codes and rules, and many topics about marriage were considered inappropriate to discuss in public. Dorothy Dix proved a big hit with her readers because she provided very un-Victorian advice. She told women to stand up for themselves and to seek practical solutions to their problems. This was radical advice to women who typically resorted to weeping and fainting in the face of difficult times.

As Dorothy Dix's popularity spread, newspaper editors around the country hired their own advice columnists. William Randolph Hearst, the owner of the New York *Journal* lured Dorothy away from New Orleans in 1901 by offering her the staggering salary of five thousand dollars.

At the *Journal,* Elizabeth continued to write her Dorothy Dix column, but she also worked as a general reporter. For one of her first assignments, she was sent to Kansas to follow and write about Carry Nation, an ardent temperance worker who was becoming famous for smashing up saloons. Nation was considered a hero by followers of the nineteenth-century Temperance Movement who were convinced drinking alcohol was the primary cause of almost all the problems in the country.

Elizabeth also covered several murder trials. Unlike the writing in her column, which was straightforward and down-to-earth, her trial stories were written in a highly emotional, "sob-sister" style. This style of writing was slanted and sensationalized, with the writer drawing her own conclusions about the case. Elizabeth once boasted that that no defendant she thought was innocent was ever convicted. But Elizabeth didn't really like writing about murder trials. She preferred writing her column and answering letters from troubled people. In 1917, when a large syndication company offered to sell her column to newspapers all over the country, she gladly accepted. She told her editor that if she ever covered another murder trial, it would be his.

Dorothy Dix became even more popular than before, and she continued writing into the mid-1900s. Besides writing her column, she lectured and wrote books that became best-sellers. She grew wealthy and purchased a large home in New Orleans. In her private life, as Elizabeth Gilmer, she worked in civic affairs and marched in women's suffrage parades. In her column, as Dorothy Dix, she advised women to obtain as much education as they could and to prepare themselves to earn their own living. But she also said that unless mothers of young children absolutely had to work, they should stay home.

Elizabeth Gilmer said that as the decades passed, she could chronicle the changes in society by the changes in her readers' letters. In the 1890s, she typically received letters from young women wanting to know if it was alright for a gentleman to come calling without a chaperone. Some sixty years later, in the 1940s, she received letters from young women asking if it was okay to go on a vacation with their boyfriends.

Elizabeth never had any children of her own, but she asked her nieces and nephews and their children to live in her mansion. While the children played downstairs, Elizabeth wrote her column in her own living quarters upstairs. Even after she was rich and famous, she always answered every letter herself. When Elizabeth retired in 1949, her column, the longest-running advice column under one author, was being read on three continents. She died in 1951 at ninety years of age.

Ida B. **Wells-Barnett**

1862–1931
Journalist, Reformer

I*t is...for the young people who have so little of our race's history recorded that I am...writing about myself.*

— IDA B. WELLS-BARNETT

Ida Wells was born a slave in the American South. But when she was six months old, Abraham Lincoln issued the Emancipation Proclamation, which promised freedom to her and all other African-Americans. As an adult, Ida did not take this promise lightly.

Ida was born in the tiny southern town of Holly Springs, Mississippi. After the end of the Civil War, her parents, who had been slaves all their lives, celebrated their freedom by entering their children in a new school established for black youngsters. But the family wasn't able to enjoy their newfound freedom for very long. In 1878, Ida's parents and one of her brothers died during a yellow fever epidemic, and sixteen-year-old Ida was left with the responsibility of supporting five younger brothers and sisters. She put up her hair to make herself look older and got a job teaching school for twenty-five dollars a month.

A few years later, she moved to Memphis, Tennessee, where she got a better job. She also took summer classes at Fisk University in Nashville so she could qualify for more advanced teaching. She rode a mule to the one-room school where she taught until she passed her teacher's exam

Once while riding a train, Ida was told to leave a first-class car occupied by white riders, but for which she had a valid ticket. Ida refused. The conductor insisted. He grabbed her arm, and Ida bit his hand! Ida was thrown off the train at the next station. Infuriated, Ida hired a lawyer and sued the railroad. She won the case and was awarded five hundred dollars. The decision was later overturned in a higher court.

After the railroad incident, Ida began writing about the increasingly unfair treatment of black people. Her articles appeared under the name of Iola, and it wasn't long before Iola was named "Princess of the Press" among the black papers in Memphis. In one article, she condemned Memphis school officials for providing inferior facilities for black students while building new schools for whites. The school board retaliated by firing her from her teaching job.

Offered a job on the Memphis *Free Speech and Headlight,* she accepted only on condition that she be allowed to purchase an interest in the paper. She shortened the name of the paper, solicited new subscriptions, and built up the circulation. Soon, she was earning a decent living from the paper's profits.

In the spring of 1892, a series of events took place that would catapult Ida from small-town to worldwide renown. These catastrophic events began when three of her African-Americans friends opened a small grocery store across the street from another store that was owned by a white man. The African-Americans ignored threats and slander and refused to close their store. Then a group of white deputies stormed into their store, and the owners, thinking they were being attacked by a mob, fired their guns and injured several men. The African-Americans were arrested and later dragged from their jail cell and taken out of town, where they were shot and killed.

Ida was livid. Despite the danger of lashing out against racism, she was

SOUTHERN HORRORS.

LYNCH LAW

IN ALL

ITS PHASES

Miss IDA B. WELLS,

Price, - - - Fifteen Cents.

THE NEW YORK AGE PRINT,

1892.

The front page of an 1888 edition of Frank Leslie's Popular Monthly

determined and fought with the only weapons she had—words. She wrote a series of passionate editorials crying out for justice. She first suggested that the black people of Memphis boycott the streetcars, and later urged them to move away, because, she said, "The city of Memphis has demonstrated that neither character nor standing avails the Negro, if he dares to protect himself against the white man or become his rival. . . . There is therefore only one thing left that we can do . . . leave a town which will neither protect our lives and property, nor give us a fair trial in the courts, but takes us out and murders us in cold blood when accused by white persons."

Ida's readers listened and followed her advice. Blacks refused to ride the city streetcars, and thousands left the city to seek better conditions in neighboring Oklahoma. These actions resulted in a tremendous loss of business in Memphis.

The night after one of Ida's strongest editorials was printed, vandals broke into her office and destroyed equipment. A note was left threatening the lives of both Ida and her partner if they ever attempted to print the paper again. Ida immediately moved to New York, where she wrote for *The New York Age,* a much larger paper and one that gave her a national audience. But now Ida used more than just the written word to fight racism. A large, forceful woman with a resonant voice and powerful eyes, Ida traveled throughout the Northeast telling people about the hundreds of innocent African-Americans being murdered and lynched in the South.

She even crossed the Atlantic, bringing her message to England, Scotland, and Wales, where she gathered the support of both blacks and whites. While all the major papers in England recognized and praised her work, in the United States she remained a hero to the black press but was mostly ignored by the major white papers.

After her trip to England, Ida moved to Chicago to write for *The Conservator,* which was owned by Ferdinand Barnett, a lawyer, editor, and politician. Ida and Ferdinand fell in love and made plans to marry, but the wedding was postponed twice due to Ida's speaking tours. One of these trips was a second trip to Great Britain, where she helped form an anti-

Ida B. Wells

25
Black Heritage USA

In 1990, the U.S. Postal System honored Ida B. Wells with a postage stamp.

lynching society. Before she left for this trip, she was hired as a special correspondent by a white paper, the Chicago *Inter-Ocean.* She wrote a column called "Ida B. Wells Abroad" about her experiences overseas.

When Ida and Ferdinand did marry, Ida demonstrated her independence and unconventionality yet again. In a move that was decades ahead of her time, she hyphenated her own name with her husband's, calling herself Ida Wells-Barnett. Ida raised six children, including two from Ferdinand's former marriage. But her family did not keep her from continuing to work for the betterment of her people.

As part of her anti-lynching crusade, she wrote two books that gave detailed statistics of the many lynchings in the United States. And, working with her husband and the respected statesman Frederick Douglass, she penned a pamphlet exposing discrimination and prejudice against blacks at the 1893 Chicago World's Fair. In 1898, she helped form the National Afro-American Council, for which she served as secretary. In 1909 she participated in the Niagara Movement, a forerunner of the National Association of Colored People (NAACP). She also organized several black women's clubs and became a leader in the women's club movement.

At the age of fifty, she began a new phase of her vigorous life by becoming Chicago's first black woman probation officer. She took part in politics and was once a candidate for the Illinois State Senate. In 1928, Ida started writing her autobiography, but she became too ill to complete it. She died three years later, at the age of sixty-eight.

In 1940, she was recognized as one of Chicago's all-time outstanding women and a housing development in Chicago was named after her. In 1970, her daughter, Alfreda Duster, completed her mother's unfinished autobiography using Ida's old notes and diaries. In 1987, in Memphis, a marker was placed at the former site of her paper, *Free Speech*. And in 1990, the U.S. Postal Service issued a stamp in tribute to this extraordinary woman.

Ida Wells-Barnett showed herself to be a unique individual from the time she was sixteen, when the responsibilities of a family were thrust upon her. Throughout her life, she was courageous and determined, fiery and militant. She spoke out loudly and forcefully at a time when most of her people were too frightened to do so, and she used her profession as a journalist to expose injustice wherever she found it.

African-American Women's Voices in Journalism

Black women in America have always faced a double challenge, discriminated against because of their color as well as their sex. In the 1850s, as the abolition movement grew, African-American journalists began speaking out. Their voices were heard through a number of small, and mostly poorly funded, black newspapers crying out for an end to slavery.

One of the first black women journalists was Mary Ann Shadd Cary, who published an abolitionist newspaper in Canada in the 1850s. Others contributed to black papers even earlier, signing their letters and articles mostly as "a young woman of color."

Though the first thrust of these women was their protest against slavery, after the Civil War they began to use the press as a forum to speak out on other topics. Women like Gertrude Mossell, Ida Lewis, and Ida B. Wells crusaded for better living and working conditions and for better education for their people.

For the most part, African-American journalists—both women and men —were largely ignored by the white press and would remain so until the second wave of the Civil Rights movement in the 1960s. Before that, most black writers spoke out through publications that were owned, operated— and read—within the segregated black community.

African-American women journalists writing for black papers in some ways found greater freedom than did their white counterparts. Black women writers were not confined to writing society news and women's fea-

Margaret Murray Washington

Marvel Jackson Cooke

tures. They covered the entire range of writing from breaking stories to politics and public affairs.

African-American women journalists were actively engaged in helping to found the National Organization of Colored Women and other organizations that worked for better education and the general uplifting of their race.

As dean of women at Tuskegee Institute, Margaret Murray Washington, the wife of Booker T. Washington, helped many young African-Americans find their way to higher education. In addition to her work at the college, Washington edited her own paper, *National Notes.*

Alice Allison Dunnigan was one of the first African-American women to become part of the Washington Press corps as White House correspondent

Daisy Bates (fourth from left) escorts some of the Little Rock students to the White House.

for the Chicago *Defender.* Dunnigan was followed in this post by Ethel Payne.

The Civil Rights movement of the 1960s opened the doors of the larger journalism community to African-American journalists. Slowly but surely, African-American women took their places among distinguished journalists. But even before that, Marvel Jackson Cooke became the first African-American woman to work as a full-time reporter for a mainstream white paper, the *Daily Compass,* in the state of New York in the 1950s.

Daisy Bates, who with her husband, owned and published the Arkansas *State Press,* came to prominence in the 1950s when she covered the hotly

Ida Lewis

contested integration of Little Rock High School in Arkansas. The Bateses were forced to close their paper in 1959, but reopened it in 1985, vowing to continue their commitment to working for improved conditions for African-Americans.

Ida Lewis, another prominent African-American journalist, was the first black woman to appear as a panelist on television's "Meet the Press." After writing for the black press for several years, Ms. Lewis became a freelancer and traveled to West Africa. Her work appeared in *Life* and other major publications. In 1970, Ms. Lewis became the editor of *Essence*. In 1972, she put up her own money to publish *Encore*. Later, Ms. Lewis established yet another publication, *Five Fifteen,* "The First Black Women's Newspaper."

Today African-American women continue to make strides in journalism, appearing more and more often on national network television news programs and as writers and columnists in newspapers across the country.

Elizabeth **Cochrane**
(Nellie Bly)

1865–1922
Journalist, World Traveler

If you have been flattered and praised, don't gulp it down wholesale. Chew it carefully before swallowing it.

—NELLIE BLY

Nellie Bly: Girl reporter. Daredevil. Star journalist. World traveler. Nellie was all of these and more. She would do anything to get her stories. Her most famous exploit was trying to beat the record of the character in Jules Verne's book, *Around the World in Eighty Days* — Nellie did it in seventy-two days. At the height of her career, she was a star of such proportion that children played with Nellie Bly dolls and sported Nellie Bly pins. At the age of twenty-five, she earned $25,000 a year — an astounding amount of money in 1890.

Nellie's real name was Elizabeth Cochran. She was born in Cochran Mills, Pennsylvania, a town founded by her father. As a child, she liked to read and write stories, but she also enjoyed playing rough-and-tumble games with her nine brothers and sisters. Like many girls of that era, she was educated at home, but she did spend one year at a boarding school when she was about sixteen.

When Elizabeth was twenty, her father died. She and her mother moved to Pittsburgh where Elizabeth tried to establish herself as a writer. But she found few editors who would accept work from a woman. Then, one day she saw an article in the Pittsburgh *Dispatch* that criticized women who dared venture into a "man's world" of work instead of staying home to care for their families. Elizabeth wrote an angry letter to the newspaper disagreeing with the article, identifying herself only as "E. Cochrane," and adding an "e" to her last name.

The editor, George Madden, invited E. Cochrane to write an article on "Girls and Their Sphere in Life," which Elizabeth did, again signing only her initial. Her article appeared in the paper, accompanied by a job offer to its unknown author—if the "gentleman" would come to the editor's office.

When an attractive young woman (rather than a man) showed up to accept the job, Madden must have been surprised, but he gave her the job. Elizabeth adapted the title of a Stephen Foster song called "Nelly Bly" for her pen name.

Nellie Bly's first story was about divorce, a topic few writers would have dared to tackle. She followed this with a series exposing the terrible conditions faced by women working in Pittsburgh's factories. While most readers found Nellie Bly's stories fascinating, factory owners threatened to stop advertising in the newspaper if they continued. Nellie was reassigned to cover society news.

But society news wasn't what Nellie wanted to write. Instead, she proposed a unique idea to her editor. She would travel to Mexico and write about life in that country. To appease objections to the dangers and unseemliness of a young woman traveling alone, she would take her mother along as her chaperone. She gave herself a crash course in Spanish and she was off. Nellie's first reports were glowing descriptions of Mexico's beautiful countryside and marketplaces filled with colorfully clothed peasants. Later, however, she wrote of the large contrast she found between the destitute lives of peasants and the opulent lives of the wealthy. She reported the story of a Mexican journalist who was jailed for writing stories against the government. Understandably, the Mexican officials were not pleased with these exposés, and Nellie had to leave the country in a hurry, smuggling the rest of her stories in a suitcase containing her underwear.

She returned to Pittsburgh but soon left to try for a job in New York. She wanted to write for Joseph Pulitzer's New York *World*, but was unable to get past the front desk for an interview. After her purse containing the last of her money was stolen, she was desperate. Legend tells that she stormed the *World*'s office and once inside, presented the editor with an irresistible idea for a story. In reality, she did not actually "storm" the office but did get inside by pretending to be a reporter for a Pittsburgh paper who wanted to interview the famous Mr. Pulitzer. She got the interview and made a pitch for a job by suggesting several ideas for stories. However, the story that was assigned to her was the editor's idea. Nellie was to pose as an insane person and get herself committed to Blackwell's Island asylum to investigate and write on conditions there. She was paid twenty-five dollars and told she would be hired as a regular reporter if she completed the assignment and wrote an acceptable story.

Practicing in front of her mirror at home, Nellie messed up her hair and perfected a wild look in her eye. Then, dressed in shabby clothes, she booked a room in a cheap boarding house. She told the proprietor she was from Cuba, and she babbled in Spanish about having lost her money and not knowing who she was. Her trick worked. The police were called, she was examined by several doctors, declared insane, and admitted to Blackwell's Island. For ten days, she experienced the appalling ways patients were treated. When she was released, the stories were a sensation and resulted in an investigation that led to improved conditions.

For the next two years, Nellie's byline appeared on the front page of the *World*. She exposed shocking conditions in factories, mistreatment of inmates in women's prisons, and graft in politics. But not all her stories were about the bad and the sad. Once she took a job as a chorus girl so she could tell her readers what the life of a dancer was like. Nellie introduced a new style of personal journalism. She wrote her stories as first-person accounts, telling her readers everything she had encountered, thought, and felt during her adventures. Soon other papers also hired "stunt girls" to find and write sensational stories, each trying to outdo the other. The stunt that ensured Nellie Bly's place in history was her whirlwind trip around the world.

Jules Verne's *Around the World in Eighty Days* was a work of fiction. His character, Phineas Fogg, floated over the earth in a balloon. At the time, there were no planes, automobiles, or fast trains, so circling the world in such a short span was thought to be pure fantasy. But that didn't stop Nellie! Readers of the *World* as well as those in many other countries followed her escapade. To publicize her trip, the *World* sponsored contests guessing the exact moment she would return. It also published games, diagrams, and daily updates following her progress.

The first step of Nellie's journey was to sail across the Atlantic. She arrived in London, crossed the English Channel, and took a train to Amiens, France, to meet Jules Verne. From France, she traveled by train, ship, donkey, and road coach across Europe and Asia. She carried her money in a bag worn around her neck. She took one suitcase, two dresses, her lucky thumb ring, a pair of heirloom earrings, and a twenty-four-hour watch to keep track of the time at home.

She marveled at the wonders of the Orient. She enjoyed rickshaw rides in China, purchased a pet monkey in Singapore, and survived a monsoon while sailing from Hong Kong to Canton, China. On the ship from Yokohama, Japan, back to the United States, the sailors wrote a poem in her honor: "For Nellie Bly, We'll Win or Die."

Crowds of cheering fans greeted her as she rode across the country from San Francisco back to New York on a special train. In New York, she was hailed with a big parade. She had traveled 21,740 miles (34,987 kilometers) in seventy-two days and eventually wrote a book about her trip.

Nellie Bly conducts an interview with an Austrian officer during World War I.

In 1895, Nellie met Robert Seaman, a seventy-two-year-old wealthy industrialist whom she married after a four-day courtship. During her marriage, she lived the life of a society matron, occasionally writing society pieces, but did no regular reporting. The marriage lasted nine years until Seaman died. After his death, Nellie took over her husband's businesses. In spite of having no experience, she ran his factories where she paid men and women at the same rates, an unheard-of innovation. She enjoyed success for a while, but a fire in the factory and dishonest employees caused her to go bankrupt. In 1914, she went to Europe, perhaps to escape the stress of bankruptcy. Unfortunately, World War I broke out and she was trapped in Austria until 1919.

She was then fifty-four and once again had to earn her own living. Arthur Brisbane, editor of the New York *Evening Journal*, and an old friend, hired her as a columnist. She continued writing until she became ill with pneumonia, from which she died when she was fifty-six. Her editor, Arthur Brisbane, said in her eulogy, "Nellie Bly was the best reporter in America."

Rheta **Childe Dorr**

1866–1948
Reporter, War Correspondent, Feminist

I am a type of all the women of my generation who have graduated out of a class into the human race.
— RHETA CHILDE DORR

When Rheta Childe Dorr made up her mind to do something, nothing stopped her. She was only twelve years old when she read in her local paper that Elizabeth Cady Stanton and Susan B. Anthony were giving a lecture on women's rights in a nearby town. Rheta wanted to go, but her father forbade it. She disobeyed him and went anyway. Rheta was so moved by what she heard that she donated her one silver dollar to women's suffrage and joined the organization. When she decided to become a journalist, she pursued her dream with the same kind of determination.

Rheta was born in Omaha, Nebraska. Even as a very young child, she acted on her own initiative. Rheta's mother once found her giving the family's clothes and linens to poor children in the neighborhood. At seventeen, Rheta entered the University of Nebraska. During her freshman year, a professor lent her a copy of Henrik Ibsen's play *A Doll's House*. The play tells the story of a woman who realizes that as long as she depends on her husband for money, she will never be considered his equal. Rheta decided that would never happen to her. She dropped out of school immediately so she could begin working toward her own economic independence.

She talked her way into a job at the post office, where she worked for two years. When she was twenty-three, she moved to New York to study art, but ended up writing stories and articles that she sold to newspapers and magazines. In 1892, she married John Pixley Dorr. They moved to Seattle, where her son was born in 1896. That same year, gold was discovered in Alaska. Seattle was the stopping place for prospectors going to and coming from the gold fields in the Klondike. Rheta roamed the streets of Seattle, talking to these prospectors. She wrote of their hopes and dreams—or disappointments and disillusionment—and sold the stories to newspapers in New York.

Rheta's husband felt her place was at home taking care of her house and child. He didn't mind her writing, but thought she should write in her spare time and stick to fiction and poetry. Rheta didn't agree. She took her son and five hundred dollars and left for New York to become a full-time journalist. This was a big step for a woman to take in 1898, but Rheta was driven by her determination.

For three years, Rheta struggled for survival because no editor would hire a woman as a full-time reporter. She made a meager living with freelance writing, and she even had to sell her engagement ring to buy food for herself and her son. Finally, she found a part-time job writing photograph captions. Then she got her big break. Theodore Roosevelt, a politician running for vice president, disliked publicity and refused to pose for photographs. Rheta was offered twenty-five dollars if she could get his picture. Roosevelt liked the spunky young woman and agreed to cooperate with the press, but only if Rheta was in charge of the camera crew.

After this, she was hired as a reporter by the New York *Evening Post* for twenty-five dollars a week. One of her first assignments was an investigative report on how difficult it was for women to find jobs in industry. Her story resulted in her appointment as chairperson on a committee for the General Federation of Women's Clubs. The committee influenced the New York government to investigate working conditions for women. Rheta was once told to write an "amusing little story" about the New York Federation of Women's Clubs. She refused, saying the work the women's clubs did was serious and she would not make fun of them.

After working hard for the *Post,* Rheta wanted a promotion and a raise. She asked her editor, who only laughed at her. He said he could hire all the women he wanted for the salary he was paying Rheta. He also told her a woman would never be considered for a promotion to editor. When she heard this, Rheta quit her job at the *Evening Post* and decided to become a foreign correspondent. With her usual spunk, she convinced editors of two papers and *Harper's Weekly* to send her to cover the coronation of the newly crowned king of Norway. In Europe, she also covered the International Woman Suffrage Alliance meeting in Copenhagen. While there, she met Emmeline Pankhurst, the English suffragist. She later helped Pankhurst write her autobiography.

Back home, in 1907, she took an assignment from *Everybody's Magazine* and once again investigated the hardships of working women. For most of a year, she traveled around the country taking jobs as a laundress, a seamstress, a clerk, and a sausage stuffer for a meat-packing plant. She discovered that women had to endure terrible working conditions and earn far less money than men for similar work. During her travels, Rheta kept careful notes but had no time to write the story. At the request of her editor, she sent him her notes. Instead of waiting for Rheta to return from her journey, the editor gave her notes to another writer who wrote the story under his own byline.

Rheta was angry and after much argument convinced the editor to include her name on the series as co-author. But when the stories came out, she was even angrier. The man had twisted Rheta's facts, and his story did not illustrate how women were being exploited. Later, Rheta wrote her own book telling her story in her own voice.

In 1912, Rheta traveled to Europe to interview feminist leaders. This renewed her earlier zeal for the women's suffrage movement, and when she returned to the United States, she led marches and made speeches promoting the cause.

In 1914, World War I was being fought in Europe, and while this war was being fought, a revolution was taking place in Russia. In 1917, the revolution was successful, and the czar of Russia was overthrown. This marked the start of the Communist era in Russia. Communism was an idea first introduced by Karl Marx in the late 1800s. He believed it was unfair that only the owners of the farms, factories, and businesses became rich while most of the people who worked for them remained poor. The basic idea of Communism was to make life better for people by having the people share in the ownership, the work, and the profits. This sounded like a good idea, and when the Communists took over in Russia, many people hoped the idea would spread to other countries.

Rheta was intrigued by Communism. She traveled to Russia for five months asking people what life was like under the new Communist government. She learned that the government and not the people owned and controlled everything. She also learned that the heads of the Communist Party became even more powerful than Russia's former ruler, the czar, had been. Despite overthrowing the czar, the people ended up with no freedom and lived in constant fear of the government. Rheta grew deeply disillusioned and no longer thought Communism was a good idea. When she returned to the United States, she wrote articles describing some of the events she had witnessed, but she had to write them from memory since the Russian officials had not allowed her to take her notes out of the country.

While she was in Russia, Rheta heard about an all-women's battalion. She spent several weeks sharing the women's wooden plank beds and accompanying them during their rigorous training. She even rode the train with them to their first battle. But when the Russian authorities found out she was an American, they refused to allow her to go any farther. That was lucky for Rheta because over half of these women were killed or wounded.

In 1918, when Rheta learned that her son, serving with the U. S. Army, was stationed in France, she asked her editor to send her there. In spite of the fact that Rheta was an accredited woman war correspondent, the French authorities would not allow her to cover war news. Instead, she joined the French YMCA and, through that organization, gave lectures about the Russian Revolution.

After returning from this trip, Rheta was struck by a motorcycle. Her injuries were so severe that it took her several months to recover. During this time, she returned to Europe, where she continued writing about world politics. In 1924, she wrote her autobiography, which told not only her personal story, but what it was like being a woman working in what was a man's world. She also wrote a biography of Susan B. Anthony, whom she had always admired. After the death of her son in 1936, Rheta became ill and retired from writing. She died twelve years later at the age of eighty-one.

Rheta Dorr's legacy to women and journalism is an important one. She was one of the first women to write hard news instead of women's news and was one of the first women accredited as a war correspondent. And along with her contemporary, Ida Tarbell, she helped set the standards for carefully documented investigative reporting.

Anne **O'Hare McCormick**

1880–1954
Editorial Columnist and Reporter

Anne O'Hare was born in England, but her parents brought her to America when she was an infant. The family settled in Columbus, Ohio, where Anne and her younger sisters attended a strict Catholic boarding school. Anne's father deserted the family when she was fourteen years old, and her mother ran a dry-goods store and sold a book of her poetry door-to-door in order to keep her children in private school.

After Anne graduated at the head of her class, the family moved to Cleveland, where both Anne and her mother worked for a small newspaper called the *Catholic Universe Bulletin.* Anne was associate editor. She stayed at this job for twelve years and then she married. For the next ten years, she spent most of her time accompanying her husband on his many business trips to Europe.

Then in 1920, when Anne was forty years old, she wrote a polite note to the New York *Times* asking if she could send them occasional articles about the interesting people she often met, such as high-ranking officials of foreign countries. Anne did not know that the publisher of the *Times* had a strict policy against hiring women. But Anne was lucky—the publisher was ill when her letter arrived, and the managing editor agreed to give Ann a chance. As it turned out, it was the *Times* that was lucky. Anne started without much formal training as a journalist, and sometimes she had to rewrite an article three or four times. But she learned quickly, and she eventually became one of the best journalists of her time.

When Anne began working for the *Times*, Europe was recovering from World War I, which had ended in 1918. But the problems across the Atlantic were far from over. Anne's articles explored the causes of these problems and warned of further turmoil to come. She continued to cover Europe through World War II (1939–45).

Anne was one of the first Americans to correctly predict that Benito Mussolini, a young Italian newspaper editor, would rise to become a dangerous figure in Italy. A skilled interviewer, she knew the importance of doing her homework ahead of time. Before her first meeting with Mussolini, she read a long, boring book on a law he had written. Mussolini was so impressed by her knowledge of his background that he came to trust Anne as a friend for many years. In similar ways, Anne gained the trust of many other world leaders, such as Winston Churchill, Adolf Hitler, Joseph Stalin, and Franklin Delano Roosevelt. Many of these men spoke to Anne even when they refused to speak with other reporters.

Anne felt people spoke more freely if she didn't take notes during interviews, so she never did. And unlike many reporters, she never tried to pry secret information from her subjects. Instead, she allowed them to choose what they wanted to talk about. As a result, her interviews provided her readers with a glimpse of the human beings behind the headlines.

Anne was first hired by the *Times* in 1921 as a stringer. A stringer is paid only for individual articles and must pay all of her own expenses connected with getting a story. In 1922, Anne was promoted to regular correspondent. She was still only paid for individual pieces, but as correspondent she also received a small weekly amount for expenses. For fifteen years, while

Anne's articles appeared constantly in the *Times*, she was still not paid a regular salary, nor was she considered a regular staff member.

Then, in 1936, her hard work paid off. She not only became a full-time paid employee, she was invited to join the editorial board as the "freedom editor." She was told to "stand up and shout whenever freedom is interfered with in any part of the world." And she did! Three times a week in her column titled "Abroad" she consistently warned of the approaching chaos in Europe. And as a member of the editorial board, she also wrote two unsigned editorials each week. Anne was the only woman on the *Times* editorial board for several years.

In 1937, she became the first woman to be awarded the distinguished Pulitzer Prize for journalism. She continued her reporting throughout World War II, following stories from one end of Europe to the other. When she was sixty-two years old, she tramped across France's muddy fields to interview U.S. General George Patton. Neither did her age stop her after the war. At sixty-nine, she scrambled up and down the mountains of Greece to cover the guerrilla war that erupted there in 1949.

In recognition of her achievements, Anne was granted honorary degrees from several prestigious universities as well as numerous journalism awards and citations from many leading women's groups. The National Federation of Press Women named her Woman of the Year in 1939, and the Overseas Press Club granted her an award as the Best Interpretive Foreign Correspondent in 1947.

In her personal life, Anne was very private. Unlike some well-known journalists, she never inserted herself into her stories. She believed that when journalists became celebrities themselves, they could not retain the objectivity she felt was essential for a good reporter. She didn't like to talk about herself and refused to grant interviews to others. She even refused, for a time, to be listed in *Who's Who*, a book that lists brief biographies of thousands of people of renown.

Many journalists, especially women, used brazen stunts and aggressive behavior to climb to the top of their profession. Not Anne McCormick.

Throughout her career, everyone who knew her, from famous world leaders to other journalists, agreed with Franklin Delano Roosevelt when he called Anne "a wonderful human being." When she died in 1954, her column in the *Times* was bordered in black and tribute was paid to her in an obituary that stated: "She understood politics and diplomacy but for her they were not the whole truth. . . . The whole truth lay in people."

The Gossip Mongers: Tellers of the Stars' Secrets

W ho doesn't like to hear a secret? Knowing secrets is fun. Especially when the secret is about somebody famous. But gossip about celebrities is more than fun—it's big business. And the people who write about the stars often become as famous as the stars themselves.

The most famous of the gossip columnists were Louella Parsons, Hedda Hopper, and Sheilah Graham. From the 1930s to the 1950s, these three women, known as the Unholy Trio, were powerful figures in Hollywood. They wrote about such big stars as Humphrey Bogart, Rita Hayworth, and Spencer Tracy. And they didn't hesitate to tell about all the shocking and scandalous things the stars did off-screen. A few words from any of these powerful women could make an unknown actor a star or ruin a current star's reputation. Because of this, the Unholy Trio were feared and hated— and at the same time, courted and wooed by actors, producers, and directors. Louella, Hedda, and Sheilah were as important to Hollywood as the stars themselves because of the publicity they provided, and they thoroughly enjoyed their power.

Louella Parsons (1881–1972) started her journalism career while she was still in high school in Illinois, working as assistant to the editor of a small newspaper. She married for the first time in her early twenties, but the marriage was not a happy one and the couple separated shortly after the birth of their daughter. In 1914, Louella took her daughter and moved to Chicago where she worked as a newspaper reporter. She also worked for

Louella Parsons

Louella Parsons (second from left) conducts a radio interview with Humphrey Bogart (left) and Bette Davis (middle).

a filmmaking company reading and writing scripts. Her career as a screen-writer was very short, but it provided her with enough background to convince a newspaper editor to hire her to author a series of articles on how to write for the movies. Louella's scripts and articles were for silent films, as talking movies had yet to be invented. She also wrote a book on screen-writing that was used as a text at Ohio State University until talking films became popular.

In 1918, publisher William Randolph Hearst hired Louella as movie critic of his New York *Morning Telegraph*. Then, in 1925 she became ill with tuberculosis, and her boss sent her to California where she could recover in warmth and sunshine. Louella loved living in Hollywood and decided to make her home there. She also decided to change the focus of her column from the films to the stars who made them. Readers enjoyed her column because it sounded like one fan talking to another—the only difference being that Louella was a fan who had the inside story on the stars' private lives.

Louella would do almost anything to get a scoop. She did not always take the time to check out the rumors she heard, nor did she hesitate to make up what she didn't know. And it wasn't only the stars' lives she told fibs about. She changed the facts about her own early life to make herself sound more glamorous.

Once she was established in Hollywood, she had no need to make her life sound glamorous. It was! She worked out of an office in her luxurious home, often talking on three different phone conversations at the same time. She invited all the most important people in Hollywood to her lavish parties, and she attended all the gala Hollywood festivities. Louella was at her peak in the 1930s and 1940s. Millions of people read her syndicated column and her articles in magazines such as *Photoplay* and *Modern Screen* and *Cosmopolitan.* They also listened to her telling the secrets of the stars on her radio show, "Hollywood Hotel."

Hedda Hopper (1885–1966) came to gossip writing not through journalism, but from the stage. Like Louella Parsons, Hedda was an early movie fan. Hedda's dream was to become an actress. This was a problem for a young girl whose Quaker family felt acting was frivolous. But Hedda didn't let that stop her! When she was eighteen, she ran away from home in Elda Furry, Pennsylvania, to pursue her dream. Hedda found her success in Hollywood, not as an actress, but as a gossip queen.

In 1913, she married DeWolf Hopper, an actor twenty-seven years older than herself, and changed her name to Hedda. Hedda appeared in her first silent movie in 1916 and tried for several years to achieve stardom. She never did. Her marriage ended in 1922, and she supported herself and her son with various boring jobs. She landed a radio job as fashion commenta-

Hedda Hopper jokes with movie star Cary Grant.

tor telling listeners who was wearing what at the horse races. She may not have become a famous movie star, but she was becoming well known and was often a guest on radio shows about Hollywood people.

In 1938, she started her newspaper column, "Hedda Hopper's Hollywood." Her acting background was an immense help to her, and from the start her column was filled with lots of inside information about the stars, the studios, and the people who ran them. Hedda quickly established herself as Louella Parsons's rival. It wasn't long before Hedda had her own radio show and was publishing articles in the big movie magazines. The competition between the two columnists provided as much gossip as did the stars about whom they wrote. Like Louella, Hedda lived in an extravagant home where she entertained Hollywood's famous stars. Sometimes

Hedda and Louella threw a party on the same night. This really presented a problem for the stars because to turn down an invitation by either of these powerful women meant running the risk of being snubbed in one or the other's column.

Hedda could often be seen at important Hollywood functions where she always wore one of her elaborate hats and kept her ears open for snippets of gossip. Unlike her rival, she kept what she heard under her hat until she could check it out. Hedda's column was known for its unerring accuracy. But although her information was accurate, Hedda was a terrible speller and she had no sense of grammar. Her method of preparing her column was to pace back and forth in her office spewing forth streams of rambling information while her secretary took notes and did the actual writing.

Hedda thoroughly enjoyed her position as a star maker/breaker. She also enjoyed living her glamorous life as friend to the big stars. She dictated her autobiography to her secretary in 1952, a story that was largely fiction. But then in 1963, she wrote another version of her own story, this time co-writing it with another author, and telling more of her true story. Hedda died in 1966 at eighty years old.

Among the Unholy Trio, the life story of **Sheilah Graham (1904–1988)** was by far the most dramatic. Much like a character in a romantic movie, Sheilah Graham truly went from rags to riches. She was born as Lily Sheil in London around 1904 (her date of birth was never verified). Her father died when she was an infant, and her mother, who worked as a cook, tried for six years to support her daughter, but was unable to. The little girl was sent to an orphanage where she was always hungry. At fourteen, she left the orphanage to care for her mother, who had become very ill.

After her mother died, seventeen-year-old Lily worked at a London department store demonstrating toothbrushes. One of her customers, Major John Graham Gilliam, offered her an office job and romanced her. They married, and Lily changed her name to Sheilah Graham. Her husband sent her to drama school, but Sheilah had little talent for acting. She was pretty and she could dance, so she tried out for—and got—parts in

Sheilah Graham

chorus lines of London shows. In addition to her theater work, she began her writing career with a romance novel and several newspaper articles about the theater. She liked the writing so much she decided to give up the stage and become a theater critic. But she thought her background would prevent her from moving in the proper social circles in England.

In 1933, she moved to the United States and landed a job as theater critic for the New York *Mirror* and the *Evening Journal.* Her column was a success, and in 1935, she was offered a syndicated gossip column and the opportunity to move to Hollywood. There, she entered into competition with the reigning queens of gossip, Parsons and Hopper. Since both of these women were known for their biting and sarcastic comments, Sheilah decided to outdo them at their own game. She quickly gained a reputation for being the nastiest of the three. But that didn't prevent people from reading her column. In fact, it probably gained her more readers. And as she became more established and gained confidence in herself, her writing became less stinging.

Sheilah's own story took another dramatic turn in 1937. By then she had divorced Major Graham and was engaged to another man. One of the guests at their engagement party was F. Scott Fitzgerald, the famous novelist and scriptwriter. Sheilah and Fitzgerald were drawn to one another like magnets. Sheilah broke her engagement, and she and Fitzgerald began a stormy love affair.

Though Fitzgerald had gained fame through his books and movies, both his life and career were in a shambles when he met Sheilah. He was separated from his wife, Zelda, who had been confined to a mental hospital for several years, he was drinking too much, and it had been a long time since he had sold a book. Sheilah helped Fitzgerald control his drinking and encouraged him to return to his writing. And he helped her. Sheilah had always felt self-conscious about her poverty-stricken childhood and lack of education. Fitzgerald, a well-educated man, designed a special course of study for Sheilah and guided her through it. Later, she wrote a book based on this course, called *College for One.*

In 1940, Fitzgerald's alcoholism killed him. Sheilah was devastated and wanted to leave Hollywood. World War II was being fought in Europe, and Sheilah asked her editor to send her to England as a war correspondent. While in England, Sheilah met and married Trevor Westbrook, with whom she had two children. By 1946 she had divorced Westbrook and had returned to Hollywood to resume her column. Sheilah had edged ahead in her competition with Hedda and Louella. Her column was carried in more newspapers than either Louella's or Hedda's. It was also featured in *Variety*, considered the most important mazagine in the entertainment industry.

During the 1950s Sheilah became even more famous. She wrote two books (one a best-seller) and a hit movie about F. Scott Fitzgerald. In the late 1960s, Sheilah was smart enough to realize that the days when Hollywood was the only home of the stars was over. Instead of focusing on movie stars, she widened the scope of her column to include celebrities from the sports world, television, and even politics. She also wrote several more books. During her last years, she lived in Palm Beach, Florida, with her grandchildren. She died in 1988 at eighty-four years old.

Helen **Rogers Reid**

1882–1970
Publisher

There are still a lot of prejudices against newspaper women . . . but newspapers . . . need the woman's point of view.

—HELEN ROGERS REID

Helen Rogers Reid's name never appeared in a byline, but in her role as vice president and later as president of New York's *Herald Tribune* she introduced innovations that brought her paper up to date and made it one of the most influential in the world.

Helen began life in Appleton, Wisconsin. The youngest of eleven children, she attended public elementary school until she was eleven years old, when she became a student at a boarding school where her brother was headmaster. Moving on to Barnard College in New York City, she thought first she would become a Greek teacher, then a zoologist. Later, her backdoor entry into the world of newspapers changed that ambition.

Though she showed no particular interest in journalism in college, in her senior year she was the business manager for her college yearbook. She demonstrated her managerial talent by being the first person ever to produce the yearbook under budget. Her Barnard classmates summed up Helen's personality in the poem they composed about her for that book:

We love little Helen, her heart
is so warm
And if you don't cross her she'll
do you no harm.
So don't contradict her, or else
if you do
Get under the table and wait
till she's through.
— BARNARD YEARBOOK, 1903

After earning her degree, Helen took a job as social secretary to Mrs. Whitelaw Reid, the wife of the publisher and owner of the New York *Tribune*. Eight years later, in 1911, she married the boss's son, Ogden. The year after they were married, Ogden's father died and he became president of the paper. Helen raised their three children (one of whom died in childhood), managed the Reid's 800-acre (324-hectare) estate, and worked as treasurer of New York's women's suffrage campaign. The $500,000 raised through Helen's efforts provided the funds for the final push that helped women finally win the vote with the passage of the Nineteenth Amendment in 1920.

Helen Rogers Reid's journalism career began in 1918, when her husband asked her to come to work at the paper to help improve the advertising department. Helen knew that women controlled 80 percent of the average family's spending, so she directed much of the advertising to women. She also believed the paper should be filled with features that appealed to women, so she added food columns, home and garden sections, literary and books sections, and other features. Due to her guidance, the paper's advertising revenues more than doubled within five years.

When she was named vice president of the paper in 1922, she recommended a merger with the paper's major rival, the *Herald*, a move that made the new New York *Herald Tribune* one of the most powerful newspapers in

President Dwight Eisenhower (front row, second from left) named Helen Rogers Reid as the only woman on an important committee that studied discrimination in government contracts.

the world. Helen succeeded her husband as president of the paper in 1947 and was chairman of the board from 1953 to 1955. Then, at age seventy, she stepped aside and her son took control.

For close to forty years at the *Herald Tribune,* Helen Reid wielded considerable influence in national politics. Her job of running an influential newspaper meant that she had her finger on the pulse of many national issues. She conferred with the most powerful leaders of industry and government, including U.S. presidents. She held weekly dinners at her home that were attended by the high and the mighty from the United States and abroad. She came to be known as "Queen Helen" for her influence and for the respect she held.

Ms. Reid was a private person who shunned publicity. She was an active athlete but also enjoyed attending the theater. One of her favorite entertainments was watching prizefights. She believed that women should work and be economically independent of their husbands and that men should take greater responsibility in the home and raising children. It was years before such ideas took hold in most American families. The many women journalists of today owe Helen Rogers Reid a measure of gratitude for opening the profession to their talents. She spent her last years at the family estate in New York and died at the age of eighty-seven.

Emma **Bugbee**

1888–1981
Reporter and Journalist

On April 22, 1962, there was a farewell party at the office of the New York *Herald Tribune*. The party was for the newspaper itself, which was about to merge with other papers. And the party was also to honor Emma Bugbee's retirement. Emma, one of the pioneers of women journalists, was ending her long career—but on the morning after the festivities, she did what she had done for the past fifty-six years. She got up, got dressed, and went to work. Though she had officially retired, she had one more story to write. Her longtime personal friend Eleanor Roosevelt had died a few months earlier and a special memorial was being presented in her honor at the United Nations. The story was not only Emma's last, but also the last one to be printed by the newspaper called the *Herald Tribune*.

Emma began working for the *Tribune* in 1910. By the time she retired in 1966, she had seen major changes, both in journalism and in the world. Emma herself was part of these changes. She took part in the suffrage marches that eventually won the vote for women. She wrote about two world wars. And it was her reporting that helped move women writers from fruit salads and homemaking into the mainstream of journalism.

Emma was born in Shippensburg, Pennsylvania, but grew up in Methuen, Massachusetts. She was named for her mother, but inherited more than a name. She also inherited her mother's strong feelings about independence for women. Emma's mother refused to wear a wedding ring because she considered it a symbol of being chained to an owner like a slave. From her father, who died when Emma was twelve years old, Emma inherited a love of classical languages. Emma studied Greek and Latin at Barnard College. Though she had no ambition to be a journalist, she joined the university press club because she thought it would be fun.

After her graduation, Emma returned to Methuen, where she taught Greek at the local high school. But when the school dropped Greek from its curriculum the following year, Emma was out of a job. A lucky break came her way. A friend who was a reporter for the New York *Tribune* wanted to take a trip to Germany. She asked Emma to fill in for her while she was gone, and when the friend decided to stay in Germany, Emma remained at the *Tribune*. For many years, she was one of only two women on the staff.

At first, Emma covered only "women's news," but as she gained experience, she covered suffrage marches, murders, flower shows, and later, politics. In 1914, Emma joined a group of suffragettes for a three-week, 150-mile (241-kilometer) march from New York City to the state capital in Albany. Each day, she slogged through the ice and snow while taking careful notes about the women's progress and about the reactions of people in the towns through which they passed. At five o'clock each day, she hitchhiked to the nearest telegraph station to send her story back to her office in New York City. The following year Emma was finally allowed to move her desk into the city room at the *Tribune*. This meant she would be working shoulder-to-shoulder with the male reporters. Until then, her desk had been in a tiny alcove on another floor.

Emma had been a reporter for four years. She was a respected member of the staff. Her desk was finally in the city room and some of her stories were appearing on the front page. But she had yet to have a byline under any of her headlines identifying her as the story's author. Her first byline came with a "stunt" story to see how generous people were. During the Christmas season of 1914, Emma donned the heavy blue coat of a Salvation Army volunteer and stood on a busy New York street corner, ringing her little bell. All through that cold day, Emma's collection kettle remained nearly empty. Her lead for her story read, "Is it the hearts or the hands of New Yorkers that are so cold?"

With the passage of the Nineteenth Amendment in 1920, the women of the United States won the victory for which they had fought so hard. They could go to the polls and vote. Since women were now voting, Emma's editor thought it was time that a woman wrote political news and sent Emma to attend the 1924 political conventions. She continued covering politics for years. In 1928, when Franklin Delano Roosevelt became president, Emma was there. As part of her story, she interviewed the new First Lady, Eleanor Roosevelt. Emma told Eleanor that she had always wanted to see the upstairs of the White House. Mrs. Roosevelt said, "Oh, I'll show you upstairs anytime. Come and have lunch with me someday."

Emma said she would love to do just that, but she had to return to New York the next day. Mrs. Roosevelt's answer was, "Well, come to lunch tomorrow and bring all the New York newspaper girls with you." Thus began Mrs. Roosevelt's famous Monday morning press conferences—held exclusively for women reporters. It was also the start of a deep personal friendship between Eleanor Roosevelt and Emma Bugbee.

From that time, Emma followed Mrs. Roosevelt wherever she went. She was with the great lady when she visited coal mines in Appalachia and when she investigated conditions of garment workers in Puerto Rico. Emma even accompanied the First Lady on a flight over Washington, D.C., piloted by Amelia Earhart. Emma also covered the Roosevelts during each of their presidential campaigns and subsequent inaugurations.

Barbara Belford, a journalist who knew both Emma and Mrs. Roosevelt, said the two women were alike in many ways. Both were warm and generous. Both did whatever they could to help other women. And both were shrewd thinkers who reacted coolly in crisis situations. Above all, both were always gentlewomen to the highest degree.

On the evening of April 22, 1966, when Emma adjusted her little flowered hat, sniffed the corsage pinned to her shoulder, and sipped champagne at the farewell party for her and the paper, it was the end of a special era of New York journalism. This was the final step in the merging of seven separate papers into one giant conglomerate. The *Herald* and the *Tribune* had become the *Herald Tribune;* the *Journal* and the *American* became the *Journal-American;* the *World Telegram* had joined the *Sun.* Now there would only be the *World Journal Tribune.*

Emma retired to a small home she had purchased in Bethel, Connecticut, where she died at ninety-three.

Judith **Cary Waller**

1889–1973
Pioneer Radio Broadcaster

One day in January 1922, Judith Waller received a telephone call. The caller asked if she wanted to run a radio station. Judith had never even heard of a radio station, and she certainly had no idea how to run one. But she agreed to try. Although the first radio broadcast in the United States had been made in 1906, only a few scientists in special laboratories heard it. It wasn't until 1920 that radio sets became available to the public and the first radio station began broadcasting. At the end of 1921, there were fewer than ten stations operating in the entire country. So it was not surprising that Judith Waller had never heard of the medium in 1922. Having accepted the challenge of becoming a pioneer in radio's infancy, Judith plunged into her job as manager of station WMAQ in Chicago. She eventually helped to establish standards and programming formats for radio, and later, for television.

Judith Waller was born and grew up in Oak Park, Illinois. After she graduated from high school in 1908, she attended a business college, then went to work for an advertising agency. Her work took her to New York, where she lived until 1920. Then her mother became ill and Judith returned to Chicago to care for her.

The surprise phone call she received in 1922 was from Walter Strong, the business manager of the Chicago *Daily News*. He told Judith his paper wanted to start a radio station in Chicago. When Judith said she knew nothing about radio, Walter assured her that no one else did either. He said they would all learn together. One of the things Judith had to learn was what kind of programming to offer. WMAQ was not the only new station in the Chicago area. Many others were starting as well. When Judith saw that most of these were featuring current popular music or jazz, she decided to make her station different. She contacted a leading opera singer, a pianist, and a violinist and convinced them to perform on the air. People liked what they heard and WMAQ became the classical music station of Chicago.

During her first year on the job, Judith also had to learn about microphones, transmitters, and all the other technical details of running a radio station. Her staff consisted of herself and one engineer. Judith was responsible for producing and directing all programming. She was also the announcer for all programs. One of her major responsibilities was finding performers and speakers. Because her station had a limited operating budget, Judith was unable to pay these people anything close to what they were worth. Instead of money, she offered free publicity in the *Daily News*. That was another of her duties—writing the ads for the paper.

As an experiment, Judith arranged to broadcast the 1924 Chicago Cubs World Series baseball games. After the broadcast, Judith received a letter from the mother of a handicapped boy. The woman said her son loved baseball, but was unable to attend the games. Judith went to see William Wrigley, Jr., the owner of the Chicago Cubs, and in 1925, WMAQ became the first station to broadcast an entire season of the Chicago Cubs' home games. Not only did Judith make one little boy very happy, but thousands of other people as well.

If baseball worked, why not football? Starting in the fall of 1924, all home games of the University of Chicago and Northwestern University football teams were broadcast to the station's growing audience.

Music . . . sports . . . what next? News! Judith decided that rather than reporting on events that had already taken place, WMAQ should broadcast live reports, while the news was happening! The Democratic and Republican conventions are held every four years. Until 1924, only people actually attending the events could hear the candidates' speeches. But radio changed that. Judith's station was one of the first to bring live coverage of political conventions to its audience.

Judith had grown to view radio as much more powerful than just a source for information and entertainment. She believed the medium held a tremendous opportunity for education. Judith pioneered educational programming with "American School of the Air," a program featuring lectures by professors from Northwestern University. Listeners could send for course outlines, discussion guides, and a photograph of each lecturer. To reach a younger audience, Judith arranged to have geography lessons broadcast directly into elementary schools as a supplement to regular classroom teaching. The first year she offered this service, only one school used it. But by the end of that year, eleven schools were tuning in.

Radio programming and formats changed rapidly in the early days. At first, the new medium carried no advertisements or commercials. Many of the early creators of radio programming believed that the cost of running radio stations and producing the shows should be paid for by the sale of radio sets. In fact, the Radio Corporation of America (RCA) began as a manufacturer of radios and set up its broadcasting stations as a means to promote sales of radios. But it wasn't long before independent stations filled the airways, and these stations needed commercials to help pay the costs of producing shows.

One of Judith's biggest programming successes was luring a local comedy team, Sam 'n' Henry, from a rival station to hers. When they moved to WMAQ, the name of the team was changed to Amos 'n' Andy. The "Amos 'n' Andy" show was a favorite in the Chicago area, and when WMAQ joined NBC's national network, it became one of the most popular shows ever to air on radio and ran for twenty years before it moved to television.

After WMAQ joined NBC, Judith became public service director in charge of educational broadcasting for the entire Midwest. In 1942, she helped set up the first university training program for careers in broadcasting, and later, she wrote a textbook on radio that was used for many years in college broadcasting programs.

In the early 1950s, television hit the airwaves and quickly began to edge out radio as the nation's most popular medium. When television arrived, Judith Waller was there. She initiated "Ding Dong School," one of the most popular early educational shows for children. The program also won the Peabody Award, one of broadcasting's highest honors.

Judith retired from NBC in 1957, but her contributions to educational broadcasting were far from over. She pioneered a special series of programs from Purdue University that were televised from airplanes to enable them to reach students in six states. She lectured at the Northwestern University School of Speech and was on the board of the National Music Camp at Interlochen, Michigan, one of the most prestigious music-education camps in the country. Though she had never attended college, Judith was awarded honorary degrees from Northwestern University, as well as many other schools of higher learning.

Sigrid Lillian **Schultz**

1893–1980
Foreign and War Correspondent

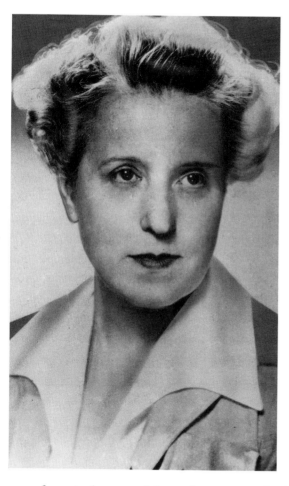

errible things were happening in Germany in 1935. Adolf Hitler had become the head of the government, and Nazism was sweeping across the country. At the same time, Sigrid Schultz was an American correspondent living in Berlin. One day, a man knocked on her door and handed her a sealed envelope. Sigrid didn't open it. Instead, she immediately tossed the envelope into her fireplace and watched it burn to ashes. Then she waited.

In a few minutes, there was another knock on the door. This time when Sigrid opened the door, secret service policemen barged into her room. Sigrid stood quietly watching them search for the envelope. When they left empty-handed, she must have smiled to herself. She had just outsmarted Hermann Göring, who was then the head of Hitler's secret police. He had hoped to trap Sigrid into being caught with secret documents. If he had, she could have been expelled from Germany.

Later that same week, Sigrid met Göring at a dinner party and gloated about how she had outwitted him. After this incident, Göring called her the "dragon lady from Chicago."

Sigrid was born in Chicago while her parents, Herman and Hedwig Schultz, were visiting the United States from their native Norway. They had come to see the World's Columbian Exposition of 1893. After Sigrid was born, her parents decided to remain and become U.S. citizens. They lived in Chicago until Sigrid was seven years old and then returned to Europe so Mr. Shultz could continue his work. He was an artist and had commissions to paint the portraits of several heads of state in Europe.

In Europe, the family made their home in France. Sigrid was educated in Paris and graduated from the Sorbonne in 1914. After she graduated, the family took a trip to Germany. They were there when World War I broke out and were unable to leave. Despite many hardships, they survived the war and decided to remain in Germany once peace came. Sigrid wanted to become an opera singer, but could not afford the lessons. So instead of practicing scales, she took a position as interpreter for a man from the Middle East who was studying at Berlin University. Sigrid's job required her to attend his classes at the university, so although she was not actually enrolled as a student, she did complete the program and received quite an education!

Her first newspaper job was as secretary and interpreter for a Chicago *Tribune* correspondent living in Germany. But Sigrid did far more than act as interpreter and secretary. Due to the many connections she had through her family, Sigrid was able to obtain interviews and stories that her boss— and other Americans—could not. Soon, Sigrid was a full correspondent. Because she had spent much of her youth in Europe and Germany, she was able to bring to her writing a perspective unique among American writers. Aside from the stories she got from the high-ranking people, she often risked her life by mingling with the crowds during riots and demonstrations to write accounts of what was happening in the streets.

Her stories were compelling, and in 1924, she became the first woman on the board of directors of the Foreign Press Club in Berlin. The following year, she joined Dorothy Thompson as one of the first women to head an American newspaper's foreign bureau. Thompson worked for Philadelphia and New York papers, and Schultz for the Chicago *Tribune.*

When Hitler became chancellor of Germany, conditions became increasingly dangerous for reporters in Germany unless they wrote only favorable things about Nazis. After Sigrid's narrow escape when she outfoxed Göring, she sometimes used the pen name John Dickson. Sigrid was committed to reporting the truth about Germany because she knew that Hitler was a dangerous force. People who knew Sigrid said they would often find her working in her tiny office late at night, fingers flying over the keyboard of her typewriter, keeping herself awake by drinking coffee and smoking a pipe. But she could not simply write her stories and mail them back to the United States. German censors read every word reporters sent out of the country, so she frequently traveled to Denmark or Norway to file her stories. She often drove at night without headlights to evade Nazi agents, who were known to follow reporters and run them off bridges.

During the 1930s, many Americans thought Hitler was a strong leader who was helping Germany recover from its defeat in World War I. But even those Americans who disapproved of Hitler did not want the United States to become involved in European politics. And no one wanted to send American soldiers to another war in Europe. In Chicago, a city with a large German-American population, pro-German feelings were particularly strong. Many of the *Tribune's* readers thought Sigrid was exaggerating the criminal aspects of the Nazis and being unfair to Hitler. But the *Tribune* supported Sigrid, and her stories continued. She wrote about Hitler's armies invading the countries surrounding Germany, and she told how the Nazi regime was terrorizing more and more people.

In 1938, Sigrid knew war was definitely coming. She sent her mother and her dog back to the United States, but she remained in Germany, where she made weekly radio broadcasts to keep listeners in Europe informed of Hitler's latest movements. Once, during a bombing attack, she was injured on her way to the radio station but still insisted on giving her report. Later, she discovered that technical problems had blocked the broadcast anyway.

In 1941, Sigrid became ill with typhoid fever and returned to Chicago to recover. She wanted to go right back to Germany but was refused a visa. During that time, she wrote a column from Chicago. In 1944, she did return to Europe—as an official war correspondent for the U. S. Air Force to cover the Allied invasion of Normandy. On May 8, 1945, when Germany surrendered to the Allied forces, Sigrid hurried to Berlin, where Hitler had been hiding in his underground bunker. Some rumors said he had escaped. Others said he had died. Sigrid interviewed a dental assistant who had recently treated Hitler. This person told Sigrid a dental bridge found in the ruins of the burnt-out bunker was definitely Hitler's. Rumors of Hitler's escape from that bunker persisted for years because his body was never found.

After World War II, Sigrid left the Chicago *Tribune* but continued to write for *McCall's* magazine and to broadcast regularly on the Mutual Broadcasting System. In 1969, she was awarded a special plaque from the Overseas Press Club recognizing her bravery and commitment to journalism. In 1977, she took part in an oral history study conducted by the American Jewish Committee in which she revealed for the first time that she had helped many Jewish people escape from the Nazis during her years in Germany. She spent her retirement years in Connecticut and died there at the age of eighty-seven.

Dorothy **Thompson**

1893–1961
Columnist and Political Commentator

> *So much truth is clouded over by propaganda and misinformation.*
>
> — DOROTHY THOMPSON

Dorothy Thompson was the scheduled speaker at a women's suffrage rally. But when she faced the audience, jeering hecklers threatened to drown her out. Dorothy hopped down from the podium and ran to a nearby store. She returned a few minutes later with a chalkboard which she held high above her head. People craned their necks to see her scrawled message: "Noise is not the truth!" Within a few minutes, the crowd quieted down and listened attentively. Throughout her life, Dorothy would show this same ability to take control of any situation she was in and turn it to her advantage.

Dorothy was born in Lancaster, New York. When she was eight years old, her mother died. Two years later her father married the organist in his church. Dorothy did not like this woman and became increasingly unhappy. When she was fourteen, still unable to get along with her stepmother, she was sent to live with an aunt in Chicago. There, Dorothy attended a private school that combined high school with the first two years of college. She was not the best student, but she excelled in languages. She was also captain of the basketball team. She entered Syracuse University as a junior with the help of a scholarship. To earn extra money, she was an ice cream vendor, a taffy puller in a candy factory, a waitress, and a door-to-door encyclopedia saleswoman. She also found time to become active in the women's suffrage movement.

Her college classmates remember Dorothy as a serious young woman who considered walking in the moonlight discussing politics and economics to be a romantic evening. She graduated from college in 1914, planning to teach, but failed the grammar section of the New York teacher's exam. Instead, she went to work for a women's suffrage group as secretary and publicist. Dorothy proved to be an excellent speaker, and it wasn't long before she was traveling around New York as spokeswoman for the organization. It was during one of these appearances that she showed her resourcefulness by using the chalkboard to silence hecklers. Dorothy also had jobs as a publicist for the Red Cross, writing copy for an advertising company, and as a social worker.

Dorothy's real ambition was to become a journalist. In 1920, there were few opportunities for women journalists, so Dorothy decided to do it on her own. With $150 and promises from a couple of editors to consider her work, she sailed for Europe as a foreign correspondent. People said that Dorothy had a great knack for being wherever something newsworthy was happening. On the ship to Europe, she met a Zionist group (people who were working to form the state of Israel) traveling to a conference in London. She spoke with them on the ship and followed them to the conference to tell their story. Her career as a foreign correspondent was underway!

In Europe, Dorothy settled in Vienna, the center of exciting changes taking place following World War I. She cultivated friends among important politicians, businessmen, writers, and artists, and became a popular hostess known for her large dinner parties. From tips she picked up from her influential friends, she sent home stories that were informative, crisp, and lively.

In 1922, she was hired as Central European correspondent for the Philadelphia *Ledger* and the New York *Evening Post* (two papers that were owned by the same company). Just a few years later she was named head of these papers' foreign news bureau in Berlin. Like Sigrid Schultz, Dorothy was one of the first American women to hold such a post.

Dorothy's stories often told of her own exploits in tracking down stories of the dangerous events occurring in Europe. And her personal life was as colorful and as exciting as the political events about which she wrote. Shortly after establishing herself in Vienna, she married Joseph Bard, a romantic Bohemian poet. But the marriage was a stormy one, and the couple soon separated.

In 1927, shortly after her divorce from Bard, Dorothy met Sinclair Lewis, a famous American author. In a story as romantic as any novel, Lewis fell in love with Dorothy over appetizers and proposed marriage to her over dessert. When Dorothy refused, he followed her through Europe and Russia until she accepted. After their wedding, Dorothy resigned her post as correspondent and moved with Lewis to Vermont. In 1930, their son, Michael, was born and Lewis won the Nobel Prize for Literature. Later, Lewis began to resent his wife's success in journalism, and this marriage, like her previous one, disintegrated.

Dorothy, now a famous writer, took frequent trips to Europe to interview world leaders. A popular speaker, she made many personal appearances as well as radio broadcasts. In 1931, when Dorothy interviewed Adolf Hitler, she was unimpressed by the strutting little man with the funny mustache. In what became the biggest blunder of her career, she wrote that Hitler was "insignificant and inconsequential." It did not take long for her to realize and admit her mistake! In a series of strongly worded articles, she warned Americans about the brutality of the Nazis and their plans to control all of Europe. Unfortunately, in the early 1930s, most Americans did not want to become involved in Europe's political affairs and were not receptive to Dorothy's message. Americans may not have been ready to listen to her anti-Nazi writing, but Hitler decided Dorothy

Thompson was too much of a threat to him. He expelled her from Germany. Dorothy proudly displayed the framed expulsion order over her desk when she returned home. She also boasted about disrupting and being tossed out of a rally of the American Bund, an organization that supported Hitler and the Nazis, in New York.

In 1936, Dorothy was considered an expert on European politics. She was a popular and widely read columnist with articles in leading magazines such as the *Saturday Evening Post* and *Cosmopolitan*. And in 1936, Helen Reid, publisher of the New York *Herald-Tribune* hired Dorothy to write a political column, "On the Record." This was another first for Dorothy—the first woman with her own editorial column. Dorothy was pleased because, as an editorial writer, she was free to interpret the news rather than simply report it. Her opinions were widely respected and in 1939, *Time* magazine called her the second most important woman in America after Eleanor Roosevelt.

Dorothy never hesitated to write exactly what she thought—even when she knew it would get her in trouble! Her paper, the *Herald Tribune*, always supported Republican candidates for president. In 1940, Dorothy supported Franklin Delano Roosevelt, a Democrat. That was her last column for the *Herald Tribune*—she was fired!

Dorothy was immediately hired by a rival paper, the New York *Post*. At the same time, she joined the Bell Syndicate, and her column was distributed to about two hundred papers and read by millions of people. She also began her weekly political commentary on the radio and wrote a monthly column for *Ladies' Home Journal* about family and home topics.

When the United States entered World War II in 1941, Dorothy was at the height of her career and popularity. In 1942, she divorced Sinclair Lewis and the next year married Maxim Kopf, an Austrian artist who had fled the Nazis. Throughout the war, she wrote of the plight of Jewish and other refugees from Europe, suggesting plans to resettle them in other countries. And she did more than write. She opened her house in Vermont as a temporary home for several of her European friends who were refugees.

After World War II, millions of Jewish refugees fled to Palestine, hoping to form a Jewish homeland. In 1948, this dream became a reality. The United Nations voted to recognize Israel as a new and separate country. But the creation of this new state brought on another war when Israel was attacked by five of its Arab neighbors. Dorothy supported the Arabs in this war instead of the Jews because she was concerned that the creation of the new Jewish state would result in millions of Arab refugees. Because of her stand, Dorothy was labeled an anti-Semite (someone who hates Jews), and her popularity plummeted. Actually, she was not an anti-Semite but was anti-Zionist—she opposed the creation of the state of Israel. She helped form the American Friends of the Middle East, an anti-Zionist organization and was elected president. But because of criticism that her credibility as a journalist would be jeopardized by being part of such a one-sided group, she resigned.

In the 1950s, Dorothy continued speaking out, voicing opinions that were not popular. At this time in America, nearly everyone was afraid of the threat of Communism. Dorothy wrote against a new law requiring government employees to take a loyalty oath. Though many people secretly agreed with her, they would not say so publicly for fear of being branded Communist sympathizers.

Dorothy's marriage to Maxim Kopf was a happy one, and when he died in 1957, she never recovered from the loss. Though she continued to write her *Ladies' Home Journal* column, she dropped her "On the Record" column. She made plans to write her autobiography, but became ill and never completed this project. In 1961, while visiting her grandchildren in Portugal, she had a heart attack and died.

Dorothy Thompson, one of journalism's most vibrant and colorful voices, left a permanent mark on her profession. Her strongly emotional writings reflected her feelings against injustice and unfairness in governments around the world. No list of prominent journalists is complete without Dorothy Thompson's name.

Mary Margaret **McBride**
(Martha Deane)

1899–1976
Newspaper and Radio Journalist

I *was sure I could write, though it was the only thing I was at all confident about.*

— MARY MARGARET MCBRIDE

During World War II, people were asked to donate scrap iron, rubber, and paper to the government for use in making badly needed supplies for the armed forces. An unusual donation came from Mary Margaret McBride, the popular host of the "Martha Deane Radio Show." When Mary Margaret heard the government needed scrap paper, she sent them more than 3 million fan letters she had stored in a warehouse!

From the mid-1930s through the 1950s, millions of people listened to Mary Margaret McBride's news commentary and celebrity interviews. At the height of her career, she was known as the First Lady of Radio and was once named one of the five most influential women in America.

Mary Margaret was born and grew up on a Missouri farm, not far from Mark Twain's hometown of Hannibal. As a young girl, she came to love books as she listened to the stories and poetry her grandfather read to her. Later, when she learned to read by herself, her grandfather kept her well supplied with books. Mary Margaret once said her best childhood friends were the characters she met in those books.

Mary Margaret attended William Woods College, a private preparatory school that was partially funded by her wealthy aunt (many private high schools at this time were called colleges). From William Woods, she went on to the University of Missouri. Her tuition was paid by the same aunt, who wanted Mary Margaret to become a teacher, and someday, headmistress of William Woods. But Mary Margaret didn't want to be a teacher, and when she insisted on majoring in journalism, her aunt stopped paying the bills. This meant Mary Margaret had to earn her own way through college, which she did by working part-time for a local newspaper.

She graduated in 1919, and obtained a position writing society news for the Cleveland Press, where she called the town's ice cream parlors to find out who was hosting the biggest parties. In 1920, she moved to Greenwich Village in New York City to work as a publicist for a religious organization. it wasn't long before she missed the excitement of reporting.

The first question asked of Mary Margaret when she applied for a job on a New York newspaper was: "Can you cover a fire?"

"You bet!" she answered. And she did! The very next week, a story she wrote about a fire was so good it was featured on the front page. Mary Margaret did well as a journalist, and her stories appeared in both newspapers and magazines such as *Good Housekeeping* and *Cosmopolitan*. Although she earned only thirty-five dollars a week at the beginning of her career, a few years later she was one of the highest-paid writers of her time.

Mary Margaret's introduction to radio came in 1934. WOR asked her to audition as host for a combination news, talk, and interview program.

Mary Margaret McBride (Martha Deane)

York radio star in 1954 and moved to the Catskill Mountains. There, she wrote a newspaper column, and made occasional radio appearances. During her career, Mary Margaret McBride was awarded several prestigious prizes for her work. She died in 1976 at the age of seventy-six.

Mary Margaret McBride (Martha Deane)

Clementine **Haskin Paddleford**

1900–1967
Food Columnist

Clementine Paddleford was only thirty-two years old when she lost part of her larynx and vocal cords to cancer. After the surgery, she had to learn to breathe and speak through a tube in her throat. It took her more than six months to master the clumsy, awkward device, and even when she did, her voice sounded strange and unnatural. But her disability did not stop her from becoming America's leading food columnist. She traveled throughout the United States and Europe speaking with housewives in markets, consulting with chefs in gourmet restaurants, and dining with kings and queens.

Clementine was born in Kansas and grew up on her parents' farm. As a child, she rose at four o'clock every morning so she could practice her piano lessons before beginning her farm chores at seven. By the age of twelve, she was an accomplished cook and often surprised her family with

The show was called "The Martha Deane Show," and Mary Margaret was supposed to act the part of a kindly grandmother who told cutesy little stories of her family while she reported news events and interviewed celebrities.

Mary Margaret thought the kindly grandmother idea was silly, but she did well on her audition and was hired. Then after only three weeks, she did something that could have cost her the job! One day, right in the middle of her show, she said her name wasn't Martha Deane and she wasn't a grandmother. In fact, she said, she wasn't a mother at all, and she wasn't even married!

The radio listeners must have appreciated her honesty because her popularity soared. Though she remained on the show for three years and continued to use the name Martha Deane, everyone knew her real name was Mary Margaret McBride. In 1940, she launched "The Mary Margaret McBride Show." Mary Margaret insisted on controlling her own show. She read all the commercials herself and refused to advertise any product she had not personally tried out. Since she neither smoked nor drank, she never advertised tobacco or alcohol.

Listening to Mary Margaret's show was like sitting at the kitchen table with a friend over a cup of coffee. She once said, "When I am on the radio I imagine that I am talking to a young married woman with a couple of children. A woman who at one time had a job and is still interested in the jobs of other people, the business world. . . ."

One of the most popular features of her program was her celebrity interviews, but Mary Margaret would never interview anyone unless she was the first to do so. She was so popular that many celebrities agreed to her terms, often waiting months for their turn on her show.

Mary Margaret was one of the first radio people to appear on television when that medium began broadcasting in 1948, but she didn't care for it and decided to remain with radio. By the 1950s, as a celebrated star, her show was broadcast from her own home, where she was able to relax and wear one of her many silk kimonos. She ended her twenty years as a New

new ways of preparing everyday dishes. She most enjoyed baking because, she said, "It smelled so good and looked the most important." At that time, though, Clementine didn't see food as her main career. She wanted to be a journalist.

Clementine's first newspaper job was writing personal ads for a newspaper while she was still in high school. She majored in journalism at Kansas State College, graduating in 1921. The next year, she enrolled in a graduate studies program at New York University. To help pay her way through graduate school, she waited tables at a restaurant, worked as a clerk in a department store, composed advertising copy, and wrote book reviews. After leaving school, she edited the women's section of *Farm and Fireside.*

Clementine had married in 1923, but was separated after only one year. She and her husband divorced in 1932, the same year she had her cancer surgery. Though that was the most difficult year of her life, she found the strength to start over again. She worked hard to overcome her self-consciousness about her disability and to make people feel comfortable despite her unusual speaking voice.

In 1936, she began what would be a thirty-year tenure as food marketing editor for the New York *Herald.* At first, she thought that writing the brief "How America Eats" column would be a part-time endeavor. But between doing her research, writing, and re-writing, she found herself working twelve hours a day. The column became much more than just recipes and cooking hints. Her readers were delighted by her vivid descriptions of foods and their cultural origins, as well as her fascinating, little-known facts about food. More than three thousand cookbooks filled Clementine's shelves, and thousands of notes, recipes, and hints sent by her readers stuffed her files. Clementine loved reading literary classics, and her writing was often filled with references from these books. She once spent months scouring Charles Dickens's books for references to food. Her research resulted in an article on preparing a Christmas dinner just like one in a Dickens story.

In 1940, she took on the additional task of writing a separate column for the *Herald*'s Sunday supplement, *This Week*. And piling work on top of work, in 1941 she began her monthly column for *Gourmet* magazine. At the height of her career, she had a following of some 12 million fans.

Clementine traveled many thousands of miles a year seeking out new recipes and stories. She shared with her readers the strange and exotic fare she was served on her trips—fresh bear meat, snake fillets, and one-hundred-year-old Chinese eggs. When she attended the coronation of Queen Elizabeth II, she gave her readers a behind-the-scenes glimpse into the royal kitchens and explained what foods were served and how they were prepared. During a trip to France, she joined royal guests at twenty-eight dinner parties hosted by France's most renowned chefs. She enjoyed both the food and the many glasses of wine that are typical in French meals, but on the airplane back to the United States, she said, "It'll be good to be home where the ice water flows like champagne."

Clementine's food column in the *Herald Tribune* was one of the longest-running single columns by one person. She wrote it from 1936 until 1966, when the paper ceased publication. Her work was twice given special recognition by the New York Newspaper Woman's Club—in 1943 and 1947. In 1953, *Time* magazine said that Clementine was the best-known food writer in America. She died in 1967.

Margaret **Bourke-White**

1904–1971
Photojournalist

A picture is perishable; [it] could vanish in a minute.

— MARGARET BOURKE-WHITE

When Margaret Bourke was ten years old, she wanted to become a herpetologist and travel to far-away jungles to study snakes. She said she wanted to "do all the things women never do." She did not become a herpetologist, but she did do many things women "never do"—at least until after Margaret did them. A pioneer in the field of photojournalism, she was the first woman accredited as a photographer for the U. S. Air Force and the first woman to fly on a bombing mission.

Margaret was born at her parents' home in New York City. The family soon moved to Bound Brook, New Jersey, where her father had taken a job as an engineer. As a child, Margaret helped her parents care for the insects and snakes they kept as pets and to study. While Margaret was close to both her parents, she was especially fond of her father, and she often visited him at the factories where he designed machinery. Even then, the young girl was filled with wonder at the stuff of industry. At home, Margaret helped her father with his hobby, photography, but it was not until after he died that she took any of her own pictures.

When Margaret entered Rutgers University at age seventeen, she planned to major in biology and engineering. The following year she transferred to Columbia University in New York City and signed up for a photography class taught by Clarence White, one of the leading photographers of the day. White taught Margaret to create a piece of art with her photographs, rather than to simply reproduce what she saw.

Margaret fell in love—with photography! She was seldom without a camera, and for the rest of her college years, she helped support herself with her pictures. After transferring to Cornell University, she took photos of the campus that helped her get her first job after college as an architectural photographer. She combined her name (Bourke) with her mother's maiden name (White) to arrive at her professional name, Margaret Bourke-White, and set up a studio in Cleveland, Ohio.

One of her first assignments was a factory set in an empty field. Margaret purchased bundles of flowers and set them around the building to create a better picture. Such meticulous attention to detail was to become her hallmark, and her work gained immediate attention from the business world, perhaps because of her ability to turn mundane subjects into works of art.

Publisher Henry R. Luce offered her a job in New York with his new magazine *Fortune*, which would focus on business. Margaret later wrote in her autobiography, "It seemed miraculous to me that these editors and I should meet and join our forces at just this time—I with my dream of portraying industry in photographs, and they with their new magazine destined to hold just such photographs." Margaret's spectacular pictures of bridges, factories, and buildings filled the pages of *Fortune*. In order to capture the full impact of the Chrysler Building, one of the first skyscrapers on the New York skyline, Margaret had herself strapped into a harness and hoisted 800 feet (244 meters) into the air. She fell so in love with New York she made the sixty-first floor of the Chrysler Building her home and studio. She filled it with her tropical fish, praying mantises (in jars), two baby alligators, and a couple of tortoises. She arranged with *Fortune* to work half of the year for the magazine, leaving the other half of the year free to take commissions to advertise tires, typewriters, nail polish, and other consumer goods.

In 1930, she traveled to the Soviet Union for *Fortune* and was the first Western photographer to document the growth of industry there. She was also the first Westerner to meet and photograph Soviet leader Joseph Stalin and his mother. Margaret wrote her first book based on her Soviet trip, and it was so popular that it made her a celebrity.

But while Margaret was enjoying her success and making big money, the United States was in the midst of the Great Depression. Thousands of people were unable to find jobs, and the farms of the Midwest were dry and barren due to a long drought. Margaret's editors sent her to do a story about the drought and its effect on the region. Seeing the desolation of the people and the devastation of the once-fertile land changed Margaret's entire perspective, both on photography and on life. Her interest turned from objects to people.

Just as Henry Luce's first magazine coincided with Margaret's desire to photograph industrial subjects, in 1935, Luce began another new magazine named *Life,* whose stories would be built around photographs of people. *Life* fit well with Margaret's changed perspective and she became one of the new magazine's first staff members and helped develop what became known as the photo essay.

Also in 1935, Margaret met the well-known author Erskine Caldwell who, like herself, wanted to tell the world how the Depression was affecting the lives of everyday people. She and Caldwell agreed to work together, and they spent months traveling through the Southern states taking pictures and talking to sharecroppers. *You Have Seen Their Faces,* the book they collaborated on, shows the stark emptiness of these people's lives in vivid detail. Many of these people lived in shacks with walls covered in old newspaper. Margaret was deeply disturbed to see on these walls her own photographs in newspaper advertisements for cars, tires, and other goods these people could never dream of owning. Margaret decided she didn't want to take pictures of luxury goods when thousands of people had barely enough money for food.

During their trip through the South, Margaret and Erskine fell in love and were later married. They wrote two more books together, and although they divorced a few years later, they remained good friends. Margaret said her life just didn't allow time for marriage.

In 1941, Margaret was in Europe covering the war. She arrived in Russia the night the Germans bombed Moscow, and her pictures of the Moscow sky embroidered with the flares and flames of German bombs are among her most memorable. When the United States entered World War II, she wanted to cover the action in North Africa, and sailed on a merchant ship because it would be safer than a troop ship. It wasn't. The merchant ship was torpedoed, and Margaret spent twenty hours drifting in a lifeboat waiting to be rescued. In order to have room for her camera, she threw out everything except one can of survival food. In Africa, she received permission to sit in the cockpit of a bomber during an air battle. The plane was hit twice, but luckily the pilot was able to get back to base.

After the war, Margaret traveled to India, where she learned to use a spinning wheel because that was the only way she could get to meet Mahatma Gandhi, the legendary leader of the Indian people. Margaret was in India when Gandhi was assassinated, and she took pictures of his funeral. Continuing her travels to capture human stories for the pages of *Life*, she climbed deep into the earth in South Africa to record the inhuman conditions under which gold was mined. She also followed American troops to Korea to record the human misery of all sides of the Korean War.

On her trip home from Korea, Margaret felt a dull ache in her arms and legs. The ache turned to increasing weakness and six years later, it was diagnosed as Parkinson's disease, a disease that destroys a person's muscles and central nervous system. Still in her mid-forties, Margaret faced her increasing disabilities with the same determination and bravery with which

One of Margaret Bourke-White's most famous photographs for Life *magazine was a portrait of concentration-camp survivors upon their release from Buchenwald in 1945.*

she had faced the rest of her life. Unwilling to admit defeat, she submitted to experimental surgery and kept up a rigorous program of exercise and therapy as long as she could. She also wrote her autobiography—first learning to type when she could no longer control a pen, and standing to do the typing when she could no longer sit. She battled Parkinson's for nearly twenty years, and when she died in August 1971, she was totally paralyzed and could only speak in a whisper.

A few days before her death, one of her friends brought her a bottle holding a praying mantis, thinking the nearness of one of her favorite creatures would comfort her. But Margaret was not comforted. She was quite disturbed and was able to communicate with her eyes what she wanted. Her friend let the insect go free, and Margaret smiled.

Margaret **Cousins**

January 26, 1905–
Editor and Writer

"Never has a magazine known an abler executive, authors a more understanding counselor, literary agents a fairer negotiator, editors a more generous associate." This quote is from a column introducing Margaret Cousins as the new managing editor of *Good Housekeeping* magazine in 1945, and it sums up what her colleagues thought of Margaret throughout her long career as a magazine editor and writer. As fiction editor for some of the country's leading women's magazines, Margaret brought readers stories by W. Somerset Maugham, Sinclair Lewis, Ellery Queen, Shirley Jackson, Edna St. Vincent Millay, A. A. Milne, James Thurber, and others. Some of these famous authors got their start because Margaret recognized their talent.

Margaret was born on the Texas prairie in 1905. Her father was a pharmacist, but he was also a writer whose short stories were published in local magazines. From her father, Margaret inherited her deep love of literature and her desire to write. She grew up listening to stories—everything from Charles Dickens and Edgar Allen Poe to the Sunday comics. By the age of four, Margaret was reading by herself, and she was writing not long after that. Her first poem was published in *Motion Picture Magazine* when she was twelve. By then, Margaret already knew she wanted to be a writer.

In 1922, Margaret entered the University of Texas at Austin, where she majored in journalism. While in college, she worked for two different magazines and was part-time editor for another. She was also the recipient of a poetry prize. After obtaining her B.A. degree in 1926, she joined the staff of *Southern Pharmaceutical Journal,* a journal published by her father. She began as an apprentice doing secretarial work and setting type, but she soon progressed to become an editor. Years later, she said, "In my journalism classes . . . I had learned a lot of notions about what would brighten up (the magazine). My father was not impressed with these notions and regularly declined my suggestions." Margaret sent articles incorporating her new notions to other pharmaceutical journals where, she said, "To my own amazement and my father's chagrin, these New York editors began to take an interest in this stuff."

Margaret's work was also being published in *Woman's Home Companion, Pictorial Review,* and other periodicals. In addition to her duties at *Southern Pharmaceutical* and her freelance writing, she also edited a quarterly professional journal published by the Drug Travelers Association. In 1936 Herbert R. Mayes, the editor of this journal, wanted Margaret to come to work for him. Margaret turned down the offer because her ambition was to work for women's magazines. The following year, Mayes again offered her a job, this time as associate editor of *Pictorial Review.* Even though it wasn't one of the women's magazines, Margaret accepted. For the next twenty-five years, she worked closely with Herbert R. Mayes, who proved to be a guiding influence on her career.

When Mayes left *Pictorial Review* to edit several magazines owned by William Randolph Hearst, Margaret followed him. Working for Hearst Publications, Margaret wrote features for *House Beautiful* and fiction for *Good Housekeeping.* In 1942 she became associate editor for *Good Housekeeping,* where she scouted for new talent, read thousands of manuscripts, interviewed and advised authors, and spoke at writers' conferences.

Another phase of Margaret's varied career opened in 1952, when she was asked to write a biography of Benjamin Franklin for children. At first she hesitated to take on this task because she had never written for children. But in spite of her fears, *Ben Franklin of Old Philadelphia* was so successful it was published in several languages and reprinted several times, most recently in 1987. She also wrote two other successful children's books.

Margaret also did a good deal of "ghost writing." When a person wants to write a book but does not have the time or skill to do the actual writing, they hire a ghost writer. Margaret provides the words for many such projects, and she also wrote stories and books under three different pen names —Mary Parrish, Avery Johns, and William Masters.

In 1961, Margaret was fifty-six years old and had been an editor and writer for thirty-five years. Her longtime mentor and friend, Herbert Mayes, tried to persuade her to give up the hands-on editing and move into the administrative end of the magazine business. Margaret was not interested. She resigned from *McCall's*, for whom both she and Mayes were working at the time, and took a job as senior editor with Doubleday Book Company.

More than two hundred of Margaret's own stories had been published in magazines, several of which were later purchased by Hollywood and television studios and made into movies. Until that time, she had never written a novel because she felt her writing was more suited to magazines. While working at Doubleday, however, she wrote a novel under the pen name Avery Johns.

Margaret was forced to retire from Doubleday when she reached sixty-five because of company policy. But she was not ready to stop working. She moved to another book company, where she helped former president Lyndon Johnson and his wife write their autobiographies. In 1971, at age sixty-six, she changed jobs again, this time to become the book editor for *Ladies' Home Journal.*

Margaret's long career as an editor ended in 1973 after she was diagnosed with rheumatoid arthritis. She moved to San Antonio, Texas, where she has lived ever since. Her first several retirement years were busy ones. She was involved in numerous educational and public service projects. She was a champion of animal rights and conservation. She helped promote literacy. She took an active role in politics. And she enjoyed storytelling. Today, she lives more quietly.

Several honors, awards, and honorary degrees attest to her prominence, as does a Lifetime Achievement Award from Women in Communications, which she revived in 1986. But of all the many awards and accolades heaped upon her, the one Margaret most values is her induction into the Texas Hall of Fame in 1986.

Dorothy Mae **Kilgallen**

1913–1965
Reporter, Broadway Columnist, TV Panelist

Dorothy Mae Kilgallen was born in Chicago, Illinois, but before she was six years old, her father's reporting jobs took the family to Wyoming, Indiana, and back to Chicago. When Dorothy was ten, her father took a position with the International News Service, and the family moved to New York.

In 1931, at the end of her freshman year in college, Dorothy attended a party with her parents where she met the editor of the New York *Journal.* When Dorothy said she would like to try being a reporter, the editor offered her a summer job. To break in his new recruit, the editor sent Dorothy to the city jail to interview thieves, pickpockets, and murderers. He also sent her to the morgue to familiarize her with seeing dead bodies. Neither the criminals nor the corpses gave Dorothy pause, and what was to have been a temporary job turned into a full-time profession. Dorothy dropped out of college and began a journalism career as a crime reporter. By the time she was twenty, she had proved herself a talented journalist and was a featured writer with her own byline.

As an adult, Dorothy looked very young and was often mistaken for a schoolgirl. She used this to her advantage. Once, when she wanted to interview the star witness in a sensational murder trial, she dressed as a teenager and knocked on the man's door. The man, who would not answer the door for other reporters, thought Dorothy was a kid from the neighborhood. Once inside, Dorothy charmed him into talking to her.

One of Dorothy's biggest scoops was her interview of Bruno Richard Hauptmann. In 1936, he was on trial for the kidnapping and murder of Charles Lindbergh's baby. Lindbergh, the first person to fly solo across the Atlantic Ocean, was one of the nation's most celebrated heroes. When his son was kidnapped and murdered, Americans were mesmerized by the coverage of Hauptmann's arrest and trial. On February 13, 1935, the trial was about to end with Hauptmann's testimony, and the entire nation wondered: Would he confess? Reporters from all over the country waited in the courtroom, notebooks in hand. Each wanted his or her paper to be the first to print the story.

Dorothy Kilgallen beat everyone to the story (including her father, who was covering the story for a competing paper). Earlier that week, she had wangled a private meeting with Hauptmann in his jail cell, where he told her exactly what he would say in court. On the day of the trial, Dorothy's story was already on her editor's desk. She had sent it to him after her meeting with Hauptmann but asked him to hold off on publishing until Hauptmann testified. The minute Hauptmann stepped down from the witness chair, Dorothy called in her go-ahead. Her story, detailing Hauptmann's confession, hit the street while all the other reporters were still writing their stories.

During her long career as a journalist, Dorothy rode in a limousine covering the coronation of Britain's Queen Elizabeth and flew around the world in a Nellie Bly stunt. And, in perhaps her most spectacular story, she interviewed Jack Ruby, the killer of Lee Harvey Oswald (the man believed to be President John F. Kennedy's assassin).

Dorothy eventually moved to Hollywood, where she began a

Hollywood gossip column, but she did not like competing with Hollywood's queen of gossip, Louella Parsons. After moving back to New York, Dorothy broke ground as the first woman columnist to cover the Broadway theater scene. Her column, "Voice of Broadway," was full of gossip and Dorothy's assessments of who were the best and worst actors. She became known for praising those actors she liked and being terribly sarcastic about those she did not. One of the actors she praised particularly highly was Richard Kollmar. In 1940, Dorothy married Kollmar and more than eight hundred people attended their lavish wedding. The year following her marriage, Dorothy began her weekly radio show with the same name as her column, "Voice of Broadway." Then, in 1945, she and her husband began a daily radio show, "Breakfast with Dorothy and Dick," which was broadcast from their home.

Dorothy had become as much a celebrity as the people about whom she wrote. Her life was a busy one. Her day began with the radio show. After the broadcast, she worked with her two secretaries on her column. Lunch was usually a celebrity interview with a Broadway star. But making time for her three children was important to Dorothy. Unless she was out of town, she picked her children up from school and took them to a park or zoo. Evenings were spent dining out with Dick or attending a Broadway opening. She seldom went to bed before three o'clock in the morning.

In 1949, Dorothy began a new phase of her career when she became a panelist on the television game show "What's My Line?" The panelists, all well-known writers or actors, guessed guests' occupations by asking a series of questions that could only be answered with "yes" or "no." "What's My Line?" was one of the most popular TV shows for nearly fifteen years.

Even though Dorothy was a famous television personality, she continued to write. In 1953, she traveled to London to cover the coronation of Queen Elizabeth. And in 1963, although it had been a long time since Dorothy had covered a sensational crime story, she joined hundreds of other reporters in Dallas, Texas, to report on John F. Kennedy's assassi-

MISS FRANCIS   MR. CERF   MISS

For several years, Dorothy Mae Kilgallen (second from right) was a regular panelist on the popular telvision quiz show "What's My Line?"

nation. Within hours of the shooting, police arrested Lee Harvey Oswald. As the police were booking him at the police station, Jack Ruby ran into the police station and shot Oswald. Ruby was arrested immediately, and Dorothy Kilgallen was the only reporter to have an exclusive interview with him. Later, Dorothy obtained a copy of the secret testimony Jack Ruby made to a special commission appointed by President Lyndon Johnson to investigate Kennedy's death. Once again, Dorothy scooped all the other reporters by publishing this information a month before the commission's public statement.

Dorothy's own death came suddenly. On the evening of November 8, 1965, she appeared on "What's My Line?" then went home. Before she went to bed, she called a messenger to take the next day's column to her newspaper office. The next morning, Dorothy's hairdresser found her dead in her bed. Medical examiners found the cause of death was an accidental overdose of alcohol and sleeping pills. Dorothy was fifty-two years old. The more than ten thousand people who attended her funeral attested to her tremendous fame and popularity.

Katharine **Meyer Graham**

1917–
Newspaper Publisher

T*o love what you do and feel it matters — how could anything be more fun?*

— KATHARINE GRAHAM

The year was 1963. Katharine Meyer Graham was a wealthy society matron who had spent the past twenty years of her life as a full-time wife and mother. Then her husband, the publisher of a journalism empire that included newspapers, magazines, and radio stations, committed suicide. Katharine was left as sole inheritor of the business. Katharine had no more planned to run a giant corporation than to become president of the United States. But she knew one thing. She must keep the company together to pass on to her children. This was a terrifying prospect for Katharine, a painfully shy woman whom somebody once described as "a shaky little doe."

The day of her husband's funeral, Katharine stood before the board of directors of her husband's empire, the Washington Post Company. Trembling with fear, she recited a carefully memorized speech assuring the men in front of her that she would never sell the company and would do what was necessary to keep the business intact. She then rolled up her sleeves and went to work. Under her guidance from 1963 to 1991, the Washington *Post* grew to become one of the most influential and powerful newspapers in the world, and the Washington Post Company became one of the country's twenty most profitable corporations.

Born in New York to a wealthy family, Katharine grew up in huge mansions surrounded by luxury, culture, and famous world figures. Katharine's father, Eugene Meyer, was a forceful businessman who had purchased the Washington *Post* and rescued it from bankruptcy. Her mother, Agnes Meyer, was a prominent social activist and well-known writer. In spite of the family's wealth, Katharine's childhood was not an easy one. She suffered from tuberculosis and spent months at a time in bed. And far worse than her illness was the feeling that she was much less capable than either of her accomplished parents—or her four brothers and sisters. She once said, "Ma did hold up almost impossible standards, and I thought everyone else was living up to them. I thought I was this peasant walking around among brilliant people."

After graduating from a private preparatory school in Virginia, she attended Vassar College and later transferred to the University of Chicago. Though her major was history, she was developing a greater interest in journalism. During the academic year, she worked on the school newspaper; during summers, she returned to Washington to work at the *Post*. This pleased her father, as she was the only one of his children to exhibit any interest in the family business. In her junior year, Katharine wrote to her sister saying she hoped one day to become a political reporter, but that she had no interest in learning the administrative aspects of running a newspaper.

After her graduation in 1938, she took an entry-level job on the San Francisco *News* for twenty-five dollars a week. The following year, at her father's request, she moved back home and joined the *Post*, working in the editorial and circulation departments. In 1939, Katharine attended a party where she met a handsome and eligible young bachelor, Philip Graham. On their first date, Philip told Katharine she would marry him. But he said he would never accept any of her father's money and that he wanted to move to Florida to become a politician. But after they were married in 1940, Katharine's time away from Washington did not last long. When Phil left to fight in World War II, Katharine returned to her job at the *Post*. When Phil returned from the war in 1945, his father-in-law invited him into the business as associate publisher. In spite of his earlier vow that he would never accept help from his father-in-law, Phil accepted the offer and began working for the *Post*. Within six months, Eugene retired, and Phil became publisher. If Katharine had been a man, Eugene surely would have handed over the business to his son, but in the 1940s, a woman was not thought to be suitable for such a position.

Katharine and Phil had four children. Much of Katharine's childhood had been spent in the care of a governess while her mother was traveling or working for one of her social causes. Wanting to spend more time with her children than her mother had spent with her, Katharine gave up her own career ambitions to devote herself to being a full-time mom. While Katharine was busy raising the children, Phil was proving to be an ambitious and dynamic businessman. He made the *Post* more successful than ever, and he expanded the company's holdings. But Phil suffered from manic depression, a serious mental illness that affected his personality. He became verbally abusive to Katharine, often making nasty jokes about her. For a long time, he carried on an affair with another woman. Though these years of her marriage were difficult, Katharine remained loyal to her husband.

In June 1963, Phil's mental illness worsened, and he was hospitalized. After a couple of months of treatment, he was thought well enough to spend a weekend at one of the family's country estates. That Sunday afternoon, while Katharine was napping, Phil shot himself in the head.

Faced with the most difficult challenge of her life, Katharine decided not to sell the paper. But she hadn't worked in more than twenty years, and she had never been involved in the management of the *Post*, let alone the other magazines and radio and television stations the Post Company owned. She had no idea where to begin, so she sought advice from trusted friends. She also drew on her own remarkable intelligence and abilities. Once she felt she had a handle on her business, she took complete charge and began making changes she felt would improve the business. Her goal was to make the *Post* one of the best papers in the country.

To do this, Katharine knew she needed the best possible person in the post of managing editor. Benjamin C. Bradlee had worked for the Post Company for years as Washington Bureau chief of *Newsweek* magazine. Katharine transferred Bradlee to the Washington *Post*. She budgeted large amounts of money for him to hire the top writers and editors in the country, and she didn't hesitate to fire those people she felt were not contributing their best efforts. Within a decade she succeeded in making the *Post* not only one of the top U.S. newspapers, but one of the most influential and powerful papers in the world.

One of her boldest moves was in 1971, when she approved publication of the Pentagon Papers, the government's secret account of the Vietnam War. The New York *Times* had already published part of these documents and was being sued by the government in an attempt to block further publication of them. Katharine's decision could have resulted in huge fines and possible imprisonment if the government successfully sued the *Post*. It was only after the papers had been published that the Supreme Court ruled in favor of freedom of the press, saying that newspapers had the right to make this information public.

Katharine scored another coup when she approved an investigative report of a burglary at the Democratic National Committee Headquarters in 1972. Her reporters, Bob Woodward and Carl Bernstein, published a series of stories that uncovered the Watergate scandal, which led to the collapse of President Richard Nixon's administration and his resignation from office in 1974. As the events unfolded, Katharine once became overwhelmed by the fact that her paper was laying bare an entire presidency and cutting to the roots of government scandal. She said, "My God, what have we done here? What's going to happen now?"

Katharine proved to be extremely astute regarding the business aspects of running a newspaper. When the company was running short of cash, she went public, or offered stock for sale on Wall Street. At first, investors were hesitant to sink money into a newspaper run by a woman. Katharine overcame her shyness to speak to a group of stock analysts and convince them she was capable of running a media empire and making it profitable. Those who listened to her were quite happy! A $10,000 investment in her company in 1971 would have grown to $185,329 by 1985.

Despite her incredible success, Katharine suffered her defeats, too. She was criticized for arbitrarily firing people she felt weren't performing as she wanted. She angered striking pressmen when she hired non-union workers to take their places. And she was cited by the Equal Employment Opportunity Commission office for not hiring or promoting more women and minorities.

In 1979, Katharine's son Donald became publisher of the *Post*. Katharine continued as chairman of the board until 1991, when Donald assumed that position as well. But Katharine did not retire. She stayed on as chief executive officer. At the time, she was one of only two women heading Fortune 500 companies. She held this position until 1993 when she was named chairman of the executive committee of the board of directors, a new position created especially for her.

In her early eighties, Katharine Graham remains active in civic, social, and journalism organizations and has received numerous awards and accolades. In 1997, she published her autobiography, *A Personal History*. For a woman who at forty-six years old was still burdened with childhood insecurities, she far exceeded her own expectations of herself. She proved herself to be an extraordinary woman and a better business manager than both her father and her husband. Television journalist Mike Wallace once said of her, "She is a woman who in effect . . . came to the job unprepared and turned out to be one the giants of journalism in the last quarter century."

Mary **McGrory**

1918–
Syndicated Political Columnist

W*hat I am is not so important as what I write.*

—MARY MCGRORY

Mary McGrory was born in Boston, Massachusetts, and is proud of her Irish heritage. She inherited her love of language from her father, who often quoted Shakespeare, but not, says Mary, in a heavy-handed way. Mary's own favorite author has always been Jane Austen. But she also enjoyed reading comic strips. In fact, her decision to become a journalist stemmed in part from her fascination with the exploits of Jane Arden, a 1930s comic-strip heroine reporter, detective, and war correspondent.

Mary attended high school at Boston's Girls' Latin School, known for its rigorous classical program. Years later another journalist praised her as the "best handler of the English language in the daily news business." Mary said that after spending four years studying Latin and diagramming sentences, "you learn how to put together a good sentence."

Mary had applied for a scholarship to Radcliffe College, but was not accepted. Instead, she attended Emmanuel College, a Catholic girls' school. She graduated in 1939 and attended secretarial school to learn shorthand and typing so she could qualify for a job at a publishing house. Hired by the publisher Houghton Mifflin, Mary's first job in the business was to crop (or cut) photographs for $16.50 a week. She moved from there to a secretarial position for the Boston *Herald Traveler*, hoping to become a reporter. The only stories she was assigned were dog and flower shows. Occasionally she wrote book reviews for the Herald.

In 1947, the book editor on the *Times* introduced Mary to the editor of the Washington *Star* who was looking for a book reviewer. For seven years, Mary reviewed books for the *Star*. She worked quietly and unnoticed, always hoping for a chance to do some real reporting. Her opportunity came in 1954 when her editor asked her to sit in on Senator Joseph McCarthy's special committee, which was investigating suspected Communist sympathizers in the U. S. Army. Mary, who was thirty-five at the time, and described herself as an ancient cub reporter, said she was terrified but delighted with her first real reporting assignment.

After sitting through the first long day of hearings, Mary wrote her story. But when she showed it to her editor, he said it was "too stiff," and told her to rewrite it. He suggested that she write as if she were talking to a favorite aunt. Mary took the advice and rewrote while thinking of her Aunt Sarah, who was old and sick but loved to read long, chatty letters. (Years later, she said she still wrote thinking of this aunt, even though the aunt had long since died.)

In the 1950s, the Soviet Union and Communism were seen as major threats to the United States. Many people, particularly writers, artists, actors—and government workers—were accused of being Communists or "Communist sympathizers" based simply on rumors. Senator McCarthy caused such fear and panic that just being summoned before his committee was enough to ruin a person's reputation. Hundreds of innocent people were "blacklisted"—they could not find work because people in their industries were afraid to hire someone believed to be a Communist.

When Mary watched McCarthy in action, she was reminded of a bully trying to terrorize people. And that is exactly what she wrote. Many people had thought this but had been afraid to speak up for fear of being branded Communist sympathizers themselves. Mary was one of the few journalists brave enough to criticize the senator in print. It was largely due to her writing that public support for McCarthy quickly died down. He was eventually discredited and left the Senate in disgrace.

After her series of reports on the McCarthy hearings, Mary was promoted directly to her paper's national desk, bypassing the more usual route of first writing for the city desk. From then on, she specialized in covering politics and in 1956, she was one of only two women journalists to cover the campaign of Democratic vice-presidential candidate Estes Kefauver. It was a grueling journey that covered thousands of miles. Mary's workdays began before breakfast and lasted into the night, when she typed her daily stories.

In 1960, Mary's column was syndicated and published in newspapers throughout the country. Mary was never the kind of columnist who obtained her material only from what was close at hand. She insisted on being on the scene of a breaking story because she felt "something would strike me that wouldn't strike anyone else." In 1979, she flew to Three Mile Island, a small community in Pennsylvania where an accident had occurred at a nuclear power plant. After seeing a photograph in a local paper showing a terrified woman running out of her house holding her baby, Mary wanted to write about the woman and her experience. But finding the woman proved to be a problem. All the people in that area had been evacuated, some to friends and relatives in surrounding areas and others to shelters and hotels. Mary took the photograph around to local shop owners, and service station attendants. She visited the evacuation centers and showed the photograph to civil defense workers. No one was able to identify the woman. Next, Mary drove through the neighborhoods affected by the nuclear accident. She recognized the house in the photograph. She noted the discarded toys left scattered in the yard, the unwatered flowers in the flower box, and other signs of a hasty departure. Finally, she learned the woman's name from a neighbor who had returned to her home. Mary sat down with an armload of local phone books, called every listing of the name, and located the woman, who was staying with a relative in a town 75 miles (120 km) away. Mary got her interview and her story. This determination to track down a story and get firsthand information was one of Mary's strengths as a journalist.

Another of her strengths was her ability to combine her clear, logical thinking with sensitivity. Never was this more evident than when her editor watched her finishing her column with tears streaming down her face on the day President Kennedy was assassinated. Still, Mary never hesitated to use her column to criticize politicians and other people whose actions she considers wrong. During the Watergate scandals, she wrote so strongly against President Nixon that she was included on his infamous "enemies list." Mary is proud of this and has been quoted as saying that it was one of the nicest things that ever happened to her.

Yet in spite of her reputation for writing the truth as she sees it, Mary was one of the most well-liked and most highly respected journalists in Washington. Throughout her career, Mary was a mentor to younger journalists, so much so that she was sometimes referred to as "Mother McGrory." For more than forty years she volunteered her spare time and energy to St. Ann's Orphanage. She sometimes snares her friends into helping out too, getting them to help with car pools or playing Santa at Christmastime. Another of her many interests was singing, which she did as a member of a choral group.

Mary McGrory has won two of journalism's most coveted awards, the George C. Polk Award in 1962 and the Pulitzer Prize in 1975. In 1997, when she celebrated her seventy-ninth birthday she was still writing her column three times a week.

Georgette (Dickey) **Meyer Chapelle**

1918–1965
Photojournalist, War Correspondent

Dickey Chapelle stepped up to the open hatch of the helicopter. On the ground far below lay a jungle deep inside enemy territory in Korea. She remembered advice that her father once gave her: "You won't fall if you don't look down. Look ahead." Looking straight ahead, Dickey stepped out of the helicopter into the hurricane-force winds tearing at her face. This was her first parachute jump, and in the coming years she would make thirty more jumps in pursuit of providing her readers with on-the-scene photographs of the war.

As a child growing up in a Quaker family, Dickey had been taught that violence in any form was unthinkable. Yet as an adult, she lived with violence on intimate terms writing and photographing war stories. Dickey was born as Georgette Meyer near Milwaukee, Wisconsin. Her parents encouraged her to think freely and form her own opinions—except about violence. Dickey and her brother were forbidden to participate in—or even watch combative sports such as boxing and wrestling. Quakers are pacifists, and pacifists refuse to engage in physical combat or war. In her autobiography, Dickey said she thought the reason she was so fascinated with war was that violence to her was a forbidden mystery.

For the most part, her childhood was pretty normal. She went to school, played with her brother and cousins, and helped out around the house. She loved the movies, especially if they were about adventures. After she saw a movie about Admiral Richard Byrd and his expedition to the South Pole, Dickey wanted to become an explorer. She also adopted the nickname "Dickey" at this time, in honor of her hero. She wanted to take flying lessons, but her mother said, "No daughter of mine is going to set foot in an airplane."

Dickey graduated from high school in 1935 when she was sixteen years old. She was valedictorian of her class and earned a full scholarship to the Massachusetts Institute of Technology in Cambridge to study aeronautical engineering. To help with living expenses at college, she accepted a job as live-in nanny to two young children. But when she was offered a part-time job as a writer for the Boston *Traveler*, she quit the nanny job and moved into a small apartment of her own.

Always fascinated with planes, Dickey spent much of her time at the naval airfield at Boston. When the nearby city of Worcester was flooded, Dickey wanted to cover the story. But she had no way to get there. Luck came her way when a pilot about to deliver relief supplies to the stricken city offered her a ride in his plane. Dickey was not only able to cover the story, but she also had her first ride in an airplane.

Between her reporting job, which she loved, and the time she spent at the airfield, Dickey neglected her studies and flunked out of school at the end of her freshman year. Back in Milwaukee, she worked as a publicist for a stunt-flying outfit. Despite her mother's fears, she took flying lessons. In 1939, she moved to New York as publicist for a major airline. She met Tony

Chapelle, the airline's publicity photographer, and took photography lessons from him. She and Tony married the next year.

When the United States entered World War II in 1941, Tony enlisted and was sent to the Panama Canal Zone. Dickey obtained a job as war correspondent for *Look* magazine and followed him to Panama. But as soon as she arrived, the army transferred Tony back to New York because of a rule against a husband and wife being in the same area during wartime. Wanting to be where her husband was, Dickey also returned to New York. Instead of working as a war correspondent, she did photo essays about unusual jobs women held during the war. She also wrote six books on aviation, two of them for young readers.

Near the end of the war, Dickey returned to the Pacific as a photographer for Fawcett Publications. She traveled on a hospital ship and photographed wounded soldiers. One day she snapped a picture of a man so horribly injured that she called her photograph "The Dying Marine." The next day, a weakened, but obviously recovering soldier greeted her as if he knew her. Dickey was amazed when he introduced himself and she realized her "dying marine" was still alive. He told her his rapid recovery was due to fourteen pints of blood he had been given. Dickey took a second picture of him and used both of her pictures in her story. These two pictures became world famous and were used as the poster for blood drives for the next ten years.

Hospital ships are unarmed, so when Dickey's ship was attacked by Japanese planes, most people on board took cover. But not Dickey! She scampered up the rope ladder to the flying bridge to snap photographs of the attacking plane.

After the war, Dickey worked as associate editor for *Seventeen* magazine. She also worked with Tony, covering stories about war refugees. In the 1950s, many women who had worked at "men's" jobs during the war found themselves out of work because so many men were returning to civilian life. Dickey was one of them. She wanted to return to Europe to continue her work as a photojournalist, but no agencies would hire a woman. So she

Georgette (Dickey) Meyer Chapelle

went on her own as a freelancer. By 1955, she and Tony's lives had taken different directions, and they were divorced.

In 1956, when Hungarians revolted against their Soviet rulers, Dickey was photographing refugees attempting to flee to neighboring Austria. She learned that medical supplies in Hungary were almost nonexistent, so she tried to smuggle penicillin into the country. Unfortunately, she was captured and thrown in prison. For five weeks, she was kept in solitary confinement. Each day she was subjected to long interrogations and was never given enough to eat. She passed the time and kept her sanity by exercising and reciting poetry.

What she had done was brave, but foolish! She had gone into Hungary without permission from anyone. This created a diplomatic problem for the United States, and American officials were unable to help her. She was finally freed after another journalist wrote about her predicament in the newspapers. Later, she wrote her own story about her imprisonment, for which she won the Reader's Digest First Person Award.

As a photographer for *National Geographic*, *National Observer*, and *Reader's Digest*, Dickey covered war stories in Korea, Cuba, the Dominican Republic, Algeria, Lebanon, Kashmir, and Vietnam.

In the early 1960s, Dickey went to Vietnam as a freelance photographer because no publication was willing to send a woman into the jungle. Her work there won her the recognition of the Overseas Press Club. They granted her the George C. Polk Award for reporting that required exceptional courage and enterprise. She also received an award from the United States Marine Combat Correspondents Association for courage and sympathetic reporting of marines in combat.

When Dickey traveled with the troops, she wore regulation fatigues but was never seen without her tiny pearl earrings. She insisted on carrying all her own equipment and asked for no special favors. The men she traveled with liked her and thought she was courageous.

On November 4, 1965, Dickey was with a company of marines near Chulai, Vietnam. As they approached the village, Dickey stepped on a land mine and was killed. Three marines were also killed that day. Dickey was one of forty-five war correspondents who lost their lives in that war. It was a bitter irony that her last article, published a few months after her death, was about the dangers of mine explosions in Vietman.

In her autobiogaphy, written in 1961, she spoke of the conflicts she faced as a journalist. One of these conflicts was feeling sympathy for the people about whom she wrote. She didn't want to exploit them, yet she also wanted to write good stories.

During Dickey's career, she was often scared to death, but she said what helped her in those moments was the motto she had learned from her father, "You won't fall if you don't look down. Look ahead." She said she thought courage consists of learning to overcome fear.

Esther Pauline "Eppie"
Lederer (Ann Landers)

AND

Pauline Esther "Popo"
Phillips (Abigail Van Buren)

1918–
Advice Columnists

Abigail Van Buren (left) and Ann Landers

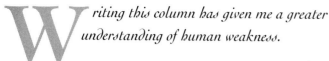

riting this column has given me a greater understanding of human weakness.

—ANN LANDERS

Most folks in Sioux City, Iowa, set off fireworks and stuffed themselves at picnics for the Fourth of July celebration in 1918. But the Friedman family wasn't at a picnic that year. They were too busy celebrating the birth of their identical twin daughters, Esther Pauline and Pauline Esther. As they grew up, the girls, nicknamed Eppie and Popo, enjoyed fooling their teachers and family by pretending to be each other. From the time they were born, Eppie and Popo were always together. When Popo became engaged and dropped out of college, Eppie did the same. They were married in a lavish double wedding in 1939. The two couples even shared a double honeymoon.

After their marriages, Eppie and Popo's lives took them in different directions. Popo's husband, Morton Phillips, stepped right into his family's successful business. Eppie and her husband, Jules Lederer, lived a much more frugal lifestyle. While Popo lived in luxury with maids and chauffeurs, Eppie did her own housework and struggled with household budgets. But Jules worked hard, and eventually he founded the Budget Rent-a-Car company. Then Eppie too, enjoyed a better standard of living.

By 1955, the twins were thirty-seven years old and had been married sixteen years. The Lederers now lived in Chicago with their daughter. Eppie was active in politics and was once elected Democratic Party chairperson for Eau Claire, Wisconsin, when they lived there. The Phillipses lived in Los Angeles with their son and daughter. Popo was active in charity and civic work. Neither of the sisters suspected that within the next few years, they would become world-famous writers.

Each of the twins is fond of telling how she got started. In 1955, Eppie saw an article in the Chicago *Sun-Times* announcing a contest to find a new advice columnist to replace the writer of the "Dear Ann Landers" column, who had died. Though she had never held a paying job, Eppie decided to enter the contest. One of the sample letters she was given to answer asked about a point of law. Since Eppie knew little about law, she called a Supreme Court justice and asked him for help. She won the contest and became "Ann Landers." Her common-sense answers, often sprinkled with droll humor, made her column popular, and it wasn't long before "Ann Landers" was syndicated in papers across the country.

In a way, Popo got her start through her sister. When Eppie began her column, she had so many letters to answer, she asked her sister to help. That didn't last long, though, because Eppie's editor insisted all the mail must be answered only by Ann Landers.

Popo decided that if Eppie could be an advice columnist, she could too. She wrote a letter to the editor of her local paper saying she could do better than the current advice columnist. At first, the editor didn't take Popo seriously, but when he read the sample columns she sent, he agreed to hire her. Like Eppie, Popo's answers were both funny and sensible. And like Eppie, Popo's columns were also soon syndicated.

This launched an eight-year feud between the sisters, as they competed with each other for outlets for their columns. Each became highly successful and each was counted among the most influential women in America. The sisters finally made up when they attended their twenty-fifth high school reunion. They have remained close ever since.

Both Eppie, as Ann Landers, and Popo, as Abigail Van Buren (a name she chose because of her admiration for President Martin Van Buren), receive mail from people all over the world. The letters come from children as young as eight and people in their nineties. About half of their letters are from men. While many letters are concerned with personal problems that seem trivial to some people, other letters ask for help in dealing with serious problems. Ann and Abby answer them all.

Unlike the early days of this century, when there were few counselors or social agencies to help people, today there are many places people with problems can go for help. But many people prefer to write to Ann Landers or Abigail Van Buren. Although most of Eppie's and Popo's answers are based on their own experience and common sense, they do not consider themselves experts on everything. Eppie has continued her practice of consulting qualified experts on behalf of her readers, a practice Popo also uses. And both columnists often advise letter-writers to seek professional help.

Sometimes, readers disagree with Ann's or Abby's answers. When this happens, they do not hesitate to write and tell the columnist she was way off base. And both Ann and Abby are quick to admit when they have goofed. Sometimes one or the other will say they deserve to be beaten "with a wet noodle."

Often, Ann's and Abby's columns become forums where people share their views and opinions. Decades ago, when Dorothy Dix and Beatrice Fairfax were the queens of newspaper advice, subjects like venereal disease, sexuality, and divorce were considered off-limits. Today, no subject is taboo in either Ann's or Abby's column. Though the scope of the problems have changed, people are still mostly troubled by family and personal problems. When Ann and Abby began their columns in the 1950s, writers worried about acne or having a date for the prom. Writers in the 1990s are more apt to seek help with problems dealing with homosexuality, AIDS, drugs, and physical or sexual abuse. Changes in their own lives have helped Ann and Abby keep pace with a changing world. Ann gained a deeper understanding of the anguish of divorce when her own marriage of thirty-six years broke up in 1975.

Today, Ann and Abby are still writing their columns every day. They each claim to have more than 90 million readers in some 1,200 newspapers.

Marguerite **Higgins**

1920–1966
War Correspondent

I had known since childhood that if there was to be a war, I wanted to be there to know for myself what force cuts so deep into the hearts of men.

— MARGUERITE HIGGINS

Within hours of Marguerite Higgins's arrival in Seoul, Korea, the city was attacked. Clutching her typewriter, Maggie hopped into a jeep full of U. S. army officers. They pushed their way through streets clogged with cars, trucks, carts, bikes, and foot traffic headed out of the city. As the jeep approached the Han Bridge, a wall of flame spread in front it. The bridge was ripped apart. One truck was blown into the air and others toppled into the river below. Maggie scrambled down the banks of the river, and helped her army companions to construct a makeshift raft. Halfway across the river, the raft sank. Still clutching her typewriter, Maggie swam to shore, then walked 20 miles (32 km) on a mountain trail to safety. A few days later, she was ordered out of Korea by a top-ranking American general because, he said, "This is just not the type of war where women ought to be running around the front lines," to which Maggie responded, "I am not working in Korea as a woman. I am here as a war correspondent."

Maggie remained in Korea and won a Pulitzer Prize for her coverage of that war. "I could not let the fact that I was a woman jeopardize my newspaper's coverage of the war," she said. Marguerite Higgins was no stranger to war. As war correspondent for the New York *Herald Tribune,* she had covered the last days of Nazi rule in Germany. That Maggie lived such an exciting life was not surprising. She wanted nothing less, and when Maggie wanted something she made sure she got it. Her desire to cover war stories stemmed from the exciting tales her father told her about his own war adventures when he was a flier in World War I in Paris.

Marguerite was born in Hong Kong, where her father and his French bride lived after the war. When Maggie was five years old, the family moved to Oakland, California, so she could attend American schools. After completing public grade school, she went to an exclusive private high school where her mother paid her tuition by teaching French classes. Maggie always appeared full of self-assurance, but at school she felt driven to prove she was as good as the more affluent students whose parents paid full tuition.

After high school, she went to the University of California at Berkeley, where she studied journalism and worked on the school paper. She graduated with honors and took a job for a local newspaper but soon left to look for a job in New York. When none were available, she enrolled at Columbia University graduate school.

Her career at the *Herald Tribune* began with her job as student correspondent. It became full-time after she obtained her master's degree. For three years, she covered general stories while she yearned to be in Europe covering World War II. In early 1944, she appealed directly to Helen Reid, the vice president of the paper. Reid gave her a post in London, where she wrote about the buzz bombs falling on that city. Her next assignment was covering Paris after the Allies had won that city back from the Germans.

Her desire for real combat action went unfulfilled until the very end of

Marguerite Higgins reports from the battlefront during World War II.

the war in Europe when she followed an army unit defeating the last of the Nazis in Germany. She learned that the reality of war was a far cry from the romantic stories she had heard from her father. Instead of excitement and glory, all she saw was the devastation of bombed-out cities and the dead bodies of young German soldiers. She did experience her own moment of glory when she reached Dachau, a German concentration camp, just ahead of the army. When she arrived, German guards—their guns at the ready—greeted her. She spoke to them in German, telling them the war was over and she was with the U. S. Army. Hearing this, the Germans surrendered their guns to her!

Maggie was only twenty-five when she was put in charge of her paper's Berlin Bureau. It was in Berlin that she met her future husband, General William Hall. In 1950, Maggie was sent to Tokyo to cover the Far East. Until she arrived in Seoul, she had thought this assignment would be too tame. Her book *War in Korea* recounted her experiences as one of the few American women correspondents in that war. During the time she was in Korea, she carried on a long-distance romance with Bill Hall. They married in 1952, but for years Bill's duties as a high-ranking general and Maggie's jaunts around the world covering news stories kept them separated for long periods.

Maggie traveled everywhere big stories were breaking. Even being pregnant didn't stop her. She accompanied Richard Nixon on his historic trip to Russia in 1954 to interview Nikita Khrushchev when she was expecting her first child.

When she returned home, the baby was born prematurely and died within five days. Losing her child was a deep blow to Maggie, and she spent months recuperating and writing her autobiography. Later, she and Bill had two more children, a son and a daughter, and after years of almost constant travel, they bought a house in Washington, D.C.

In 1965, Maggie made what would be her last journey to the Far East, visiting Vietnam, India, and Pakistan. On her return from this trip, she became ill. At first the doctors could find no explanation of her symptoms, but finally diagnosed her as having a rare and fatal tropical disease called leishmaniasis, which is caused by the bite of a sandfly. It is believed she contracted the disease in Vietnam. By a strange twist of fate, this was the same disease that had killed her maternal grandfather, who also contracted it in Vietnam while fighting with French forces in the early 1900s.

Maggie faced her death with the same uncompromising stubbornness with which she had faced everything else in her life. She refused to give in until the very end but died on January 3, 1966.

Helen **Gurley Brown**

1922–
Magazine Editor

Use your guts and energy to inspire yourself, your job, your intellect, and every other possible thing.

— HELEN GURLEY BROWN

Helen Gurley Brown's story is an American Dream come true. Unable to afford college, she enrolled in secretarial school. In a period of thirteen years, she held seventeen different jobs. She remained single until she was thirty-seven years old, then married a movie producer who suggested she write a book based on her own experiences. Her book was a hit and made her a celebrity. She then catapulted into the publishing world and she eventually transformed *Cosmopolitan* into one of the most influential magazines of the century.

Helen was born in Green Forest, Arkansas, a small town in the Ozark Mountains. Both of her parents were schoolteachers who stressed the importance of education. When Helen was seven years old, the country was plunged into the Great Depression. Her parents, who had always been poor, became even poorer. But Helen's mother, who made clothes for Helen and her older sister, always taught Helen to "look her best." Much tragedy was to come to Helen's family. Her older sister was stricken with polio, which left her confined to a wheelchair. And when Helen was ten years old, her father was killed in an elevator accident. After the accident, Helen, her mother, and her sister moved to Los Angeles, where she attended high school and spent her free time reading movie magazines. Though she did well in school, she was filled with insecurities and had a low opinion of herself. She was, she says, too skinny, had a "terminal" case of acne, and was terrible at sports.

After high school, Helen studied shorthand and typing, and she obtained a secretarial job at a local radio station for six dollars a week. She quit a few months later because her boss kept yelling at her. Helen was no different from thousands of other young women. She didn't think of her job as a career, but just as a way to earn money until she met the "man of her dreams" who would carry her off to "happily ever after."

After years of bouncing from one job to another and finally becoming serious about her work as an advertising writer, Helen did meet the man of her dreams. His name was David Brown, and he was a movie producer. When they met, David was married for the second time, and in the process of divorcing. Their friends probably gave this unlikely match little chance of success, but they were wrong. Helen's marriage has lasted thirty-eight years and is still going strong.

David suggested to Helen that she write a book about her years of struggles as a single woman in the working world. The book, *Sex and the Single Girl*, proved to be an instant best-seller. Soon enough, Helen used her husband's business connections to land a job as an editor with *Cosmopolitan*.

Helen says that in the years before her phenomenal success she was a "mouseburger," a word Helen invented, meaning a woman of average intelligence and average looks who has neither a superb education nor social connections. A mouseburger lacks confidence in herself but has drive and the ability to work hard. Helen proved this when she took over as editor-in-chief of *Cosmopolitan*. The magazine had been around since 1883, but by

1965, it was losing money and appeared hopelessly dated. Though Helen knew nothing about running a magazine, she knew what kind of magazine would appeal to single working women. Instead of filling her magazine with recipes and household tips, she sought articles that helped women make the most of their looks and talents.

Helen learned the publishing industry as she went along. At first, she tried to do everything herself, taking home piles of work each night. One of Helen's most important lessons was learning to assign work to her staff. Helen discovered she was a good administrator and negotiator, and it wasn't long before she had a staff who respected her. She also discovered she was an excellent editor and could write a snappy column herself.

Some people thought the "Cosmo Girl" image promoted by Helen placed too much emphasis on makeup and looks. In the 1970s, feminists believed the magazine should stress issues such as equality in the workplace instead of concentrating on dating and fashion. But Helen pointed out that *Cosmo* did promote independence and assertiveness in women and that being feminine doesn't mean being weak. By the 1980s, both the women's movement and *Cosmo* had changed. The feminists were less militant, and *Cosmo* contained articles discussing serious topics written by people like Betty Freidan and Gloria Steinem, two longtime leaders of the women's movement.

In the three decades that Helen Gurley Brown headed *Cosmopolitan*, she won special awards from the University of Southern California and Stanford Schools of Journalism and was inducted into the Publishers' Hall of Fame. In 1986, the Hearst Corporation, which owns *Cosmopolitan*, funded the Helen Gurley Brown Research Professorship at Northwestern University Medill School of Journalism. Until she retired as *Cosmo* editor-in-chief in 1997, Helen wrote her "Step into my Parlor" column every month. If there was one message that she repeated in that column, it was: "If I could do it, so can you!"

Liz **Smith**

1923–
Gossip Columnist

Did gossip columnists disappear when the last of the "Unholy Trio" stopped writing? Not by a long shot! Hollywood may no longer be what it was in the 1930s and 1940s, but there are still plenty of stars—movie stars, television stars, sports stars, and others. And people still thirst for inside information on the private lives of famous people.

Today's top gossip columnist is Liz Smith, whose syndicated column appears in hundreds of newspapers. But unlike her predecessors, Liz does not wield her power in quite the same way. Where Louella Parsons, Hedda Hopper, and Sheilah Graham were known for their cutting remarks and for putting people down, Liz is known for her friendliness and kindness. Another difference between Liz Smith and the others is that from the beginning of her career, Liz was a serious journalist.

Liz was born in Texas and recalls her childhood as a warm and loving, but strict one. She says she grew up between the Travis Avenue Baptist Church and the Tivoli movie theater. Both were influential in her life.

When she was young, Liz wrote fan letters to movie stars Tom Mix and Ginger Rogers. She also wrote and made up her own newspapers. She eventually majored in journalism at the University of Texas, where she once wrote a story about the actor Zachary Scott. She sent the story to Scott, who liked it so much that he offered to help Liz find a job when she graduated. Liz didn't really intend to specialize in writing about Hollywood or stars, so she thanked Scott and continued her studies.

In 1948, Liz graduated from college and moved to New York, but she was unable to find a position as a journalist. When she realized that Zachary Scott lived in New York, she remembered his offer. He introduced her to the editor at *Modern Screen* magazine. Liz was on her way.

After working for *Modern Screen,* she was an associate producer on Mike Wallace's radio broadcasts and for the television show "Wide, Wide World." Then she got a job writing a gossip column for the New York *Journal-American,* but not under her own name. In 1964, she became entertainment editor for Cosmopolitan, and later was a staff writer for *Sports Illustrated.* She also wrote articles for several major magazines such as *Ladies' Home Journal, Vogue,* and *Esquire.*

In 1975, Liz was hired to write her own gossip column for the New York *Daily News* syndicate. The editor chose her because of her friendly tone and her sense of humor. He said he was tired of the old-style gossip columns in which the writer typically tried to be as nasty as she could. At first, Liz wasn't sure she wanted to do a gossip column. She had hoped to write hard news. But she couldn't resist the huge salary and the opportunity to have her own featured column in a major newspaper.

When Liz's first column appeared in 1976, she had few celebrity contacts, but she spent hours on the phone, did a lot of background reading, and made sure she met important people. Her readers liked her and often sent her tidbits of information she could use. It wasn't long before she was scooping the other gossip columnists, nor was it long before her column was increased from three to six days a week.

Today, besides her column, Liz appears regularly on television and is known for her down-to-earth sense of humor. Liz writes on a computer in her home office. While she writes, her three telephones ring off the hooks, and her cats doze in her letter basket. When her column is finished, she sends it to the newspaper by modem.

Even though Liz spends much of her time with glamorous people, she considers herself just an ordinary person. She once told an interviewer from a food magazine that her favorite food is Campbell's Tomato Soup and that she loves microwave popcorn and Snickers bars.

Erma **Bombeck**

1927–1996
Humor Columnist, Author

> *You just keep writing and writing and writing and rewriting and rewriting.*
>
> — ERMA BOMBECK

For more than thirty years, Erma Bombeck's column, "At Wit's End," was a must-read for thousands of devoted fans. She kept her readers chuckling about hungry washing machines that ate socks, kids who fought over the last cherry in the fruit cocktail, and dogs with bad breath. Erma didn't write about problems facing world leaders. She wrote about the frustrations faced by ordinary people in everyday life. Her readers loved her column because it helped them laugh at themselves and relax.

Erma was born in Dayton, Ohio. Her father, Cassius Fiste, who had worked as a laborer, died when Erma was nine years old. After that, it was up to Erma's mother, who had only a fourth-grade education, to support the family. Mother and daughter moved in with Mrs. Fiste's parents, and Mrs. Fiste found work in a factory.

In spite of her family's difficulties, Erma's childhood was a happy one.

She lived in an ethnically mixed neighborhood and had friends that came from many different backgrounds. On Saturday mornings, Erma attended services at a Jewish synagogue with one friend; on Saturday evenings, she attended a revivalist tent meeting with another friend; and on Sunday mornings she attended Catholic church with yet another.

Erma was a shy child, so her mother found the money to enroll her in a tap-dancing class, hoping this would help build her daughter's self-confidence. It did. While in grade school, Erma sang and tap-danced for local radio stations.

Erma always liked to make people laugh. She wrote her first humor column for her school paper in the eighth grade. Even at such a young age, Erma knew she wanted to become a professional humorist. She studied the writings of James Thurber, Max Schulman, and other funny writers to better learn her craft. Once she started writing, Erma never stopped. She continued writing for her school paper through high school and also wrote a newsletter for a local department store.

By the time she graduated from high school, Erma knew she wanted to do her writing in newspapers. She enrolled in college but had to drop out because she couldn't afford the tuition. But Erma did not give up her dream. If she couldn't enter journalism with a degree, she would begin at the bottom and work her way up. She took a job as a copy-girl for the Dayton *Journal-Herald*. While still working for the *Journal-Herald*, she returned to college and also wrote for her college paper. In 1949, she obtained a B.A. in English and began working full-time for the *Journal-Herald*. That same year, she married William Bombeck, whom she had met several years earlier when he was working as a copy boy for a competing newspaper. Erma and William would later adopt a daughter and then have two sons of their own.

Erma didn't get to write a humor column for the *Herald* right away. For five years, she wrote obituaries, a few women's features, and weather reports—which she says was her first experience at writing fiction. But her journalism career was interrupted when she began having children. Like most American women in the 1950s, Erma gave up her career to be a full-time mother.

But after years of motherhood, Erma felt frustrated being bound to household chores. When her youngest child entered school, Erma said, "I do not feel fulfilled cleaning chrome faucets with a toothbrush." She suggested a weekly humor piece to the editor of her local paper. He agreed and paid her three dollars for each column. Using herself and her own family for source material, Erma wrote her first columns on a typewriter perched on the edge of her bed, often in the midst of normal family turmoil.

Her column was popular with her readers, but only reached a small audience. Two years later, the editor of her old paper, Dayton *Journal-Herald*, offered her a job in which she could reach a larger audience. Erma was an immediate hit. Her editor sent a sample of her column to a national syndicate, and within a few weeks, Erma's column was being read by people in cities across the country. Erma was on her way to becoming famous!

Since she wrote about the woes of housework and raising children, she thought she was appealing mostly to housewives, but it turned out that men got as many chuckles from her writing as women. Once, she was invited to speak to 3,500 farmers' wives in Kansas City. Nine thousand people showed up—men as well as women.

In addition to writing her column, for several years Erma kept up a hectic schedule traveling around the country as a featured speaker. In 1971, she wrote the first of her eleven books, most of which were on the best-seller list for months. For eleven years she was regularly featured on ABC's "Good Morning America." In the early 1980s, she cut back on her speaking engagements because she wanted more time at home with her family.

Erma once said her column was supposed to sound "like something that came off the top of my head as I was folding the laundry." But her writing was actually very hard work. She often rewrote an article many times to perfect it. She once said that when she filled out forms asking for her occupation, she listed "rewriter."

Erma may have played down her incredible skill, but her popularity proved her extraordinary talent. Her column appeared in papers in more than seven hundred cities, and for several years she was listed among the twenty-five most influential women in America. She was a member of President Jimmy Carter's National Advisory Committee for Women, was the first woman elected to the American Academy of Humorists, and was honored with many other special awards and honorary degrees.

In 1990, Erna was diagnosed with breast cancer and had a mastectomy (the removal of a breast). The medication she had to take during that illness aggravated a hereditary kidney disease she had battled all her life. For the next five years, she spent part of each day hooked to a dialysis machine which did the job her own kidneys were unable to do. Then, in 1996, she underwent surgery for a kidney replacement. Unfortunately, complications set in, and she died. But throughout her medical ordeal, Erma's writing reflected a realistic, yet sunny, approach to life. In a column written shortly before her death, she wrote, "Lighten up! Don't take life so seriously."

Barbara **Walters**

1931–
Television Journalist

As a young child, Barbara Walters dreamed of becoming a famous actress. She never became an actress, but she has certainly become famous. Barbara is, in many ways, the First Lady of television. She was the first woman to deliver "hard" news on network television and the first woman television journalist to command a million-dollar salary. For more than two decades she has co-hosted the popular magazine show "20/20" and her own "Barbara Walter's Specials." She has interviewed presidents, dictators, generals, movie greats, sports giants, and even condemned murderers on Death Row.

Barbara grew up surrounded by famous people, so perhaps it is not surprising that she has always felt comfortable around them. Her father was the founder and owner of the Latin Quarter, one of New York's most famous nightclubs. Many of the celebrities who visited the club were also guests in the Walters's home. Though Barbara was born in a suburb of Boston, Massachusetts, most of her childhood was divided between New York and Miami Beach, Florida. Barbara knew the glamorous life her parents lived was not the way most people lived. She once described her home as a "huge castle." Though she lived a privileged life, she had few friends and often felt lonely and shy around people her own age.

She attended a Miami Beach public high school for a time but graduated from a private prep school in New York. She then studied at Sarah Lawrence College, where she obtained a B.A. in English in 1953.

As a teenager, Barbara had given up her dream of becoming an actress and had decided to become a teacher instead. While studying for her master's degree in education, she worked as secretary for an advertising agency. Later, she took a job as assistant to the publicity director at a television station. In the early 1950s, television was still a fairly new medium. It was exciting and challenging, and Barbara was there when it all began. Her desire to teach ended when she was one of the few people selected to participate in a special training program for television producers.

One of her first professional positions on television was as a writer-producer for the Dick Van Dyke and Jack Parr shows. That job ended in 1957 when she was fired as part of staff cutbacks. Barbara wanted to continue working in television, but she didn't want to remain backstage. She asked Don Hewitt, at that time a producer on CBS, if he thought she would be good on camera. He told her, "You're a marvelous girl, but stay out of television."

Barbara believed him. "I was the kind nobody thought could make it. I had a funny Boston accent. I couldn't pronounce my R's. I wasn't a beauty." She left television and worked in public relations for theater companies. This began what Barbara has called her "dark ages years." Not only was she unhappy with her work, but during that time, she entered into a bad marriage that was annulled within a few months.

Things picked up for her in 1961 when she was hired as a writer for NBC's "Today" show. Then she was chosen as part of a group of journalists to accompany First Lady Jacqueline Kennedy on a trip to India. When Barbara returned, she did her first on-camera feature about the trip.

At this time, women were seldom given "serious" spots on television news programs because the producers felt they didn't sound authoritative. Women journalists had long fought the prejudicial belief that their writing voices lacked authority. When television came on the scene in the 1950s, women faced even more hurdles in acceptance. Not only did they have to sound authoritative, they had to look good on camera. This meant that women were automatically disqualified for on-camera jobs unless they were attractive, a prejudice that continues today. And this led to a further bind. Attractive women were not seen as "serious" or intelligent.

By the mid-1960s, the tradition among most news and talk shows was to include pretty women to make entertaining small talk. The "Today" show always featured one such woman, called the Today Girl. Every time NBC hired a new Today Girl, Barbara would think, "Hey fellas, look at me, I'm right here, how about me?" But she was too shy to say it out loud. Then Hugh Downs, the host of the show, told Barbara she could fill in on a trial basis. Barbara was thrilled, but she did not want to appear pretty-but-stupid. During her years behind the scenes, she had honed her skills as a serious journalist, and she wanted to be seen as such. NBC officials thought the audience would not react well to a woman presenting serious news, but Barbara proved them wrong. Her professionalism in handling interviews was immediately apparent, as was her ability to do straight news reports. Barbara remained as co-host of "Today" for fifteen years.

In 1976, Barbara shocked the nation when she left NBC to co-anchor the nightly news with Harry Reasoner on ABC. This was a tremendous break-through, not only for Barbara, but for all women in broadcast journalism. It was the first time a woman was featured as an anchor of a major network newscast. But the year proved a difficult one for Barbara. She faced a great deal of opposition from the station's top executives and from her male col-leagues. And aside from having to deal with problems in her career, her second marriage was ending in divorce, and she was facing life as a single mother.

Despite her problems, Barbara forged ahead in her career. Soon after moving to ABC, she launched her "Barbara Walters Specials"—hour-long

Barbara Walters has interviewed countless celebrities and world leaders. Here, she poses tough questions to former President Richard Nixon in 1980.

programs in which she interviewed top celebrities. Her specials were so popular that the next year she gave up her position as anchor and concentrated on doing her special interviews and a series of investigative reports. She later began co-hosting "20-20" with Hugh Downs, her former colleague on the "Today" show. The TV news magazine is consistently one of the top-rated shows, and it places Barbara Walters before the nation on a weekly basis. Today, she is considered the top interviewer on television and one of the most prestigious journalists in television history—female or male. Among her many honors, Barbara has won an Emmy Award for excellence in television broadcasting.

Barbara's rise to the top may look as if it were an easy one, but she had to overcome a great many obstacles to get there. First there were her own insecurities that she wasn't "good enough." Then there were the very real barriers against women in television. And perhaps most of all, she had to make extreme sacrifices in her personal life. She has had three unsuccessful marriages, and has raised her daughter on her own.

Asked about her strengths and weaknesses, Barbara once said she was a good interviewer and a good editor. She admitted she was impatient and sometimes compulsive. She is easily bored, very ambitious, and demands extremely high standards from her staff — sometimes, she says, too high. Others agree that she is demanding, but note that Barbara demands no less of herself than she does of her staff. When asked what was most important to her, Barbara said, "To feel valued, to know, even if only once in a while, that you can do a job well."

Georgie Anne **Geyer**

1935–

Foreign Correspondent and Syndicated Columnist

Georgie was born in Chicago, Illinois, in what she calls a rough neighborhood with a bully on every block. When she was very young, she nicknamed herself GeeGee, a name she still uses. Always interested in writing, Georgie wrote a novel when she was ten years old. By the time she graduated from high school at sixteen, she knew she wanted to be a journalist. This was a surprise to her family, who expected her only to marry young and raise a family.

Georgie attended the Medill School of Journalism at Northwestern University. During her junior year, she spent three months studying in Mexico. After her graduation in 1956, she won a Fulbright Scholarship for further study in Vienna, Austria. While overseas, she had her first taste of revolution. In 1956, Hungary revolted, unsuccessfully, against the rule of the Soviet Union, and Georgia got a close-up view of the dramatic events.

When Georgie returned from Europe, however, her life was put on hold. She had a severe case of hepatitis and was in bed for an entire year. She says that year taught her patience—a necessary trait for any reporter. After recovering from her illness, Georgie obtained a position as society reporter for the Chicago *Daily News*. A couple of years later, she asked her editor for a more meaningful assignment. She was sent undercover to act as a waitress at a big Mafia dinner. She picked up all sorts of information, and her story won an award from the Chicago Newspaper Guild.

Next came the event that truly changed her life. On a whim, she applied for a special grant allowing her to work in Latin America because she had held a deep interest in the region. She had visited Cuba with her parents when she was fifteen, vacationed in the Andes mountains, and studied in Mexico during college. She was fascinated by the people and their cultures.

When her six-month grant expired, Georgie became her paper's only Latin American correspondent. In the mid-1960s, many Latin American countries were run by dictators who ruled with strict laws and kept their people in poverty. In some of these countries, the people revolted by arming citizens, organizing them into groups of soldiers called "guerrillas," and carrying out surprise attacks on government soldiers and buildings.

Georgie did what no other American journalist had done when she made contact with guerrillas in Guatemala and traveled with them for three days. Georgie lived with the fear that she could be killed at any moment by her companions or by the government forces the guerrillas were fighting. She accompanied them as they hiked through jungles and across mountains in the middle of the night. In quiet moments, Georgie got what she was after. She spoke with the soldiers, learning firsthand the poignant stories of their difficult and sometimes tragic lives under a fierce government.

Georgie covered many other Latin American revolutions during the 1960s and 1970s, frequently spending long periods living with the people and learning their points of view. Some Latin American dictators were supported by the United States government as a way of protecting American business interests. But Georgie never hesitated to criticize American policy when she felt it was wrong. This made her the target of much criticism herself. Still, Georgie became known as the United States expert on Latin America.

Georgie Anne Geyer conducts an interview in Latin America in the 1970s.

Georgie was a Chicago *Daily News* foreign correspondent for eleven years. During that time, up to 75 percent of her time was spent flying from one country's revolution to the next. She admits to doing some foolish things to get stories, things that put her in grave danger. She loved the sense of excitement, and she felt it was her mission in life to explain foreign cultures to her American readers.

In 1975, she changed her job from foreign correspondent to columnist, writing through the Los Angeles *Times* syndicate. She says she knew it was time to switch when she began to think about the danger she was in. Her job title may have changed, but her life stayed much the same. She continued to travel to troubled countries and to interview their leaders. She also continued to flirt with danger. In 1976, she was thrown into prison in Angola, Africa, because the authorities didn't like what she wrote. Among the many world leaders she has interviewed are Jordan's King Hussein, Libya's Muammar Gadhafi, Iraq's Saddam Hussein, Palestine's Yasir Arafat, and Israel's Shimon Peres.

Rather than bombarding her subjects with questions, Georgie takes a more passive approach. By encouraging her subjects to speak freely, she says she seldom has to ask questions. Learning to be a good listener, she says, is one of the most important skills a journalist must have. Another is patience, especially for a foreign correspondent. "Waiting around," says Georgie, is much of what a foreign correspondent does—waiting for travel connections, waiting to make contacts, waiting for appointments—or just waiting for a story to break.

In 1983, Georgie wrote her autobiography, *Buying the Night Flight,* which a colleague of hers said should be required reading for aspiring foreign correspondents. In the book Georgie talks about what motivated her to specialize in covering rebellions and revolutions. She says she always loved to write, had a hatred of injustice and corruption, and an intense curiosity about the world. She was able to combine everything she loved by writing about the struggles of those trying to free themselves from oppressive governments.

Today Georgie continues to write her column. She is also a regular panelist on "Washington Week in Review," a TV news program on PBS. When she is not traveling, she lives alone in her Washington, D.C., apartment, which is decorated with the clutter of twenty-three years of world travel. She has never married because her hectic life never allowed time to form a close, lasting relationship.

Georgie often finds herself in the role of mentor to young journalists. Her advice to these young people is, "There is only one thing I really know. . . follow what you love in life. You say you don't know what you love? Easy. Experiment and find out, and gradually, but honorably, dismiss the things from your life that are not so important."

The Second Wave: From Women's Rights to Women's Liberation to Human Rights

Equality of rights shall not be denied or abridged by the United States or by any state on account of sex.

—FROM THE PROPOSED ERA AMENDMENT

From the time Mary Wollstonecraft, a British author, wrote, "I do not wish [women] to have power over men, but over themselves," in 1792, women have been fighting for their rights. The early suffragists fought a bitter struggle to win the right to vote from the mid-1800s to 1920. When the Nineteenth Amendment was passed in 1920, many activists believed their job was done. But in reality, their work had just begun.

The right to vote did not really change women's lives. While there were always those few who broke from tradition, most women were still expected to marry and raise a family—and not much else. Women seeking employment were offered mostly low-level positions. In schools, they were often denied admittance to graduate level studies, and thus shut out of most professions. In private life, unmarried women past their mid-twenties were labeled "old maids" and considered too old to marry. Married women were supposed to obey their husbands, who were legally the heads of the households. Married women were unable to obtain credit in their own names, so they had little or no economic power. Some men thought that being head of the household included the right to enforce their position with violence. Women who were beaten by their husbands were offered no legal protection.

Society was gradually changing, however. Throughout the 1920s and 1930s more women sought employment outside the home, and more women became involved in political and social organizations. During World War II, thousands of American women took on jobs that were vacated when men went off to war. By the end of the 1950s, many people were questioning the longtime belief that a woman's role is to be a wife and mother and to assist her husband. Then came the 1960s, a time of activism and protest. Millions of citizens protested the U.S. government's decision to send American soldiers into the war in Vietnam. Martin Luther King Jr. led the push for civil rights for African-Americans and other minority groups. And then came the second wave of the women's rights movement.

In 1963, Betty Friedan's book, *The Feminine Mystique,* spoke about millions of housewives who felt they had no control over their own lives. She wrote about women who had excellent capabilities and education, but were still denied any opportunity to move ahead in the business world. Friedan pointed out that women had been taught for generations that their only acceptable roles were as wives and mothers. Under Friedan's leadership, women began meeting in what were called "consciousness-raising" discussion groups. As women shared their experiences and feelings, the new women's movement began.

The movement received a big boost with the passage of the Civil Rights and Title VII acts of 1965. Both laws protected all people, regardless of color or sex, against discrimination in the workplace and in public places. But having a law on the books doesn't mean it is always followed. The National Organization for Women (NOW) was formed in 1966, led by Betty Friedan. The group's goal was to win full economic equality for women.

When Gloria Steinem joined the women's movement a few years later, she wanted NOW to work for more than economic equality—she wanted it to work toward changing people's basic attitudes. Many feminists were concerned with the way language influences people's thoughts and attitudes. Linguists (people who study language) began to examine the effect of using male words such as "he" and "man" to stand for all human beings. They also questioned the use of words such as "chairman" and "mailman" because they implied that only a man could perform these jobs.

It wasn't only language that contributed to people's attitudes toward women. Many people felt that if children in school read only about families where the mother stayed home and the father went to work, that would seem to be the way families should be. As a step toward changing basic attitudes, children's schoolbooks began to use the word "she" more often. They also portrayed families where both parents worked and both parents took an active part in caring for the children and the house.

Gloria Steinem wanted NOW to campaign for women to have total reproductive freedom over their own bodies. She urged both women and men to take precautions to avoid unwanted pregnancies, but also argued strongly for a woman's right to choose to have an abortion. Many people in the movement did not agree with this. In the early 1970s, as had happened earlier in the suffrage movement, there was much disagreement among the women leading the movement. Yet, in spite of the dissension, NOW became larger and gained much influence. One result was more women running for public office.

In 1972, the Equal Rights Amendment (ERA) to the Constitution, which had first been introduced to Congress back in 1923, was re-introduced. This time the resolution did pass Congress, but could not become a law until it was ratified by thirty-eight out of the fifty states within ten years. Some opposed the ERA because they were afraid it would mean the end of separate rest rooms for men and women. Others were afraid women would be drafted into the military. Still others felt the ERA was no longer needed because a variety of other laws protected against sexual discrimination.

A backlash movement, led by Phyllis Schlafly, argued that women should rejoice in their "natural" role of motherhood and helpmate to a man. Schlafly's group campaigned vigorously against the ERA, and by 1982, the ten-year limit for ratifying the ERA had passed. The amendment died.

In the 1980s, many people said the women's rights movement had died as well. In fact it was not dead, but it had changed. It focused on continuing to change society rather than on just examining and discussing issues (as it had in the 1960s and 1970s). So many changes have now taken root in society that young people growing up in the 1990s may not realize just how different things are today than they were a few decades ago. And the changes have benefited not only women, but men as well. Today, both women and men have the freedom to work in any field in which they have ability. Women are employed as mechanics, pilots, engineers, and other occupations which were once considered appropriate for men only. Fifty years ago almost all nurses and elementary schoolteachers were women. Today, male nurses and male elementary teachers are serving thousands of people.

But there is much yet to be done. The focus in the 1990s has been on continuing progress in economic and career opportunities for women. And another focus has been on stopping domestic violence and sexual harassment. It is only within the past decade that any progress at all has been made in this area. Sexual harassment lawsuits against highly placed individuals and even against institutions have helped increase public awareness in these areas.

Though women in the workplace today fare far better than their predecessors, they have not yet achieved total equality with men. In many fields, women earn less than men even when their jobs are the same. Women are beginning to move into executive and managerial positions, but in large corporations, few women make it to the highest levels. As we move into the twenty-first century, hopefully this, too, will change.

Gloria **Steinem**

1934–

Journalist, Editor, Leader of Women's Movement

In 1968, Gloria Steinem wrote entertaining articles that appeared in leading magazines. One day she was assigned to cover a meeting of women protesting New York's restrictive abortion laws. That meeting changed the direction of Gloria's life because for years she had been living with a secret—that she had undergone an abortion. The abortion rights meeting helped to open Gloria's eyes to the women's movement as well. After that meeting, Gloria realized the women's movement was not only for unfulfilled married women—it was for all women. Gloria never again wrote fluffy entertainment pieces. Instead, she became an outspoken feminist, and she helped a new generation of women fight to gain the social, economic, and political equality they had always been denied.

Gloria was born in Toledo, Ohio, in the midst of the Great Depression. For the first several years of her life, her family traveled around the country eking out a living selling antiques and junk at flea markets. During these years, Gloria's mother, Ruth, suffered from depression, which became increasingly worse. When Gloria was ten years old, her parents separated. Her father moved to California, and she and her mother lived in a run-down area of Toledo, Ohio.

After her father left, Gloria's childhood came to an abrupt end. Instead of being cared for by her mother, she became her mother's caretaker. There was an older sister, but she was married and had a family of her own. On days when her mother was particularly bad, Gloria stayed home from school. Her one pleasure during this period was tap-dancing. She was good at it and sometimes performed at neighborhood parties. Her dream at that time was to turn professional and dance her way out of her dismal life.

She didn't dance her way out, but in her senior year of high school, her older sister came to her rescue. She brought Gloria to live with her in Washington, D.C., and obtained medical help for their mother. Gloria finished high school and applied for college. Though her grades were low, she did well on the entrance exams and was admitted to Smith College in Massachusetts.

In college, Gloria studied government. For the first time in her life, she led the carefree life of a student. She made many friends and even became engaged to marry. But when she was offered a chance to study in India, she broke her engagement. Later, when asked why, she said, "In the 1950s, once you married, you became what your husband was, so it seemed like the last choice you'd ever have."

But the problem was that Gloria was pregnant. She was afraid that if she had a child, the same thing would happen to her that had happened to her mother. She had always felt that her mother's illness came, in part, from never having the chance to fulfill her own ambitions. Her mother had been a newspaper reporter but had quit her job when she married. Without ever telling anyone about her predicament, Gloria terminated her pregnancy by having an abortion in England on her way to India.

While in India, Gloria was deeply touched by the terrible poverty and discrimination she witnessed. She decided to become a journalist and write about the problems she saw in society, hoping in that way, to help bring about changes. But on her return to the United States, she was unable to find any magazine or newspaper willing to hire a woman to do serious writing. She moved to Boston, where she was co-director of the Independent Research Service, an offshoot of the National Student Organization.

Gloria's journalism career began in 1960, when she moved back to New York. Still unable to find a job writing about social change, she wrote instead about celebrities, fashions, and other lighthearted topics. During her spare time, she worked for the civil rights movement. In 1963, Gloria donned a skimpy costume, attached a pair of bunny ears to her head and a fluff of cotton to her backside. She was posing as a Playboy Bunny at a popular men's club. With a plastic smile pasted on her face, and her aching feet encased in high heels, she served drinks and gathered information for an undercover article. Even though the article emphasized the humiliation faced by Playboy Bunnies, most people saw it as another bit of froth.

The next few years were profitable for Gloria. She wrote a best-selling book about tips for sunbathing and was a scriptwriter for a popular television comedy show, "This Was the Week That Was." She also wrote for many top magazines and became known as one of the glamorous, unmarried career girls in New York.

While her writing was mostly light entertainment, in her personal life she campaigned for liberal political candidates and worked for causes such as helping Cesar Chavez in his fight to obtain better working conditions for agricultural workers in California. She said that during this period she felt she was living a double life. Then, in 1968, she helped found *New York,* a magazine for which she wrote a monthly political column.

While gathering material for her column, she attended the 1968 abortion-rights meeting that so changed her life. As Gloria listened to women at the meeting talk about the dangers and degradation they had experienced when they sought abortions, Gloria recalled her own experience. She realized that if women were ever to gain the right to truly control their own lives, they had to have a voice.

Gloria became that voice. She spoke at women's clubs, college seminars, and civic groups. She organized consciousness-raising "cells," where women gathered to discuss their shattered dreams and frustrations. These groups were far more than gripe sessions. They were open forums that helped women realize that only if they worked together, could they hope to change things. Gloria also wrote articles about women's issues but few magazines would print them. That's when a new idea was born.

If other magazines would not deal with women's issues, then Gloria would create a magazine that did. Her editor at *New York* magazine promised financial help. Gloria and a few other women, working out of Gloria's cramped apartment, put together a sample issue. They named their new publication *Ms.* Why *Ms.*? Gloria used the term to emphasize that all men were called "Mr." whether they were single or married, and women were called "Mrs." if they were married and "Miss" if they were not. *Ms.* was the first magazine dedicated solely to women's issues since those of the early suffragists. And it was the only magazine fully owned and run by women.

The first issue of *Ms.* was distributed as an insert in a special issue of *New York*. Nobody knew if people would be interested in a "feminist" magazine. To everyone's surprise—most of all, Gloria's—more than 300,000 copies of the first full issue were sold within a few days. Soon, thousands of women were using the title Ms. in front of their names instead of Miss or Mrs.

Gloria remained a full-time editor of *Ms.* until 1987, when the magazine was sold to an Australian company. Since then, she has spent her time writing, acting as consulting editor for *Ms.*, and working for various causes. Aside from continuing her work for women, she has become increasingly involved in working with Native Americans in this country and native cultures of Africa. She has never married and still lives in the same New York apartment where the first issue of *Ms.* was born.

Gloria once said, "The point is not the choice(s) we make. The point is to make a choice." The women's movement has helped to make it possible for women to make those choices.

Cokie **Roberts**

1943–
Broadcast Journalist

Politics is in Cokie's blood. Her father, Thomas Hale Boggs, was a Louisiana congressman for many years. In 1972, the plane on which he was a passenger disappeared and was presumed to have crashed in the snowy wilds of Alaska. After the accident, Cokie's mother, Corinne, ran for and won her husband's position, which she held until 1990. Cokie's sister was mayor of Princeton, New Jersey, and her brother is a Washington attorney and lobbyist. So it's no wonder that Cokie, too, is interested in politics. As a lead correspondent for both ABC news and National Public Radio, she is today one of the nation's leading political reporters. Legendary newsman David Brinkley once said about Cokie: "She knows more about Congress than any single member [of Congress] knows . . . and ten times more about it than I ever did."

Cokie was born in New Orleans, Louisiana, and spent her childhood there and in another home her parents kept in Bethesda, Maryland, just outside of Washington, D.C. Cokie's given name is Mary Martha Corinne

Morrison Claiborne Boggs. Her mother called her "Pooh Bear" after Winnie the Pooh, and her brother, who couldn't pronounce Corinne, nicknamed her "Cokie."

As children, Cokie and her siblings were encouraged to share in dinner-table political discussions. Many families talk politics, but in the Boggs home, dinner guests often included some of Washington's most powerful politicians. From an early age, Cokie had the chance to sharpen her wits against members of Congress, and even presidents. But Cokie says she really learned about politics from her mother, who ran her father's campaigns.

Cokie attended a Catholic girls' high school, where she edited the school paper, and then went on to Wellesley College, where she obtained a B.A. in political science in 1964. Her first job after graduation was as an assistant producer and hostess of a local television program.

In 1966, she married Steven Roberts, a journalist for the New York *Times*. Among the 1,500 guests at their wedding were President Lyndon Johnson and most members of Congress. Though she was earning more money than Steven, Cokie gave up her job and moved to New York because that was where Steve worked. For eight months, Cokie looked for a journalism position at newspapers, radio, and television stations. To her dismay, most job interviews didn't touch on her journalistic skills—most people just asked how quickly she could type.

Cokie finally did find work as an editor and later as a producer for a television station. When Steve's job took him to Los Angeles, Cokie once again left her job to follow him. She says the turning point in her own career came in 1974, when she accompanied her husband on his assignment to Athens, Greece. Cokie was working as a part-time correspondent for CBS radio and was on the scene when George Papadopoulos, the head of Greece's military government, was overthrown. When Cokie reported live from Greece, it was the lead story of the night, and Cokie realized how much she enjoyed the excitement of being in the center of the action.

When she returned to the United States, she was recruited as a news

Cokie Roberts talks politics on "This Week with David Brinkley."

announcer by National Public Radio (NPR). Before she went on the air, she was told her nickname was "too flip" (casual) and that she should use her given name. But when Cokie recited her full name, Mary Martha Corinne Morrison Claiborne Boggs Roberts, her boss changed his mind.

Cokie eventually became NPR's Capitol Hill correspondent. Her congresswoman mother sometimes provided Cokie with inside tips, but it was Cokie's perceptive reporting and sharp wit that made her a favorite with NPR's listeners. In 1981, Cokie made her first regular appearances on television as co-host of Public Broadcasting System (PBS) show "The Lawmakers." A few years later, she joined the staff of the highly respected "MacNeil-Lehrer News Hour," also on PBS.

Even though Cokie was well on her way to becoming a television news personality, she continued her affiliation with NPR. She said that in some ways, radio was easier—she could do the broadcast from her home wearing her pajamas. There were problems, though. One time her basset hound's persistent barking disrupted a live interview she was conducting.

Cokie was a regular on both public radio (NPR) and public television (PBS). But when ABC invited her to become a regular panelist on "This Week with David Brinkley" and the political correspondent for "World News Tonight," she was in a unique position. Never before had a journalist worked for both a public and a commercial station at the same time. "This Week with David Brinkley" was the leading Sunday-morning news show on television. The program drew the top Washington politicians and featured lively debates among several journalists, including Cokie. But during her first appearances on the show, the other panel members—all men—would talk to each other and not to her. Cokie was concerned that if she interrupted them, the audience would think her too aggressive and hard. On the other hand, if she was polite and waited her turn, she would look like a wimp. Drawing on her childhood memories of heated discussions around the dinner table, she became a "determined interrupter."

Cokie was quickly accepted, and television viewers across the country recognize her as an authority on Washington politics. She is a popular lecturer and often writes articles for the country's leading news magazines. She has received many awards for her work and has been named one of the country's most successful and influential women.

In 1995, in Atlanta, at a special ceremony honoring her mother's political accomplishments, Cokie noted that more women today hold political office than ever before. She said, "I think women today find it more acceptable to be straightforward about holding power." That applies to women in all fields, not just politics, and to Cokie as much as to her mother.

Charlayne **Hunter-Gault**

1942–
Broadcast Journalist

I n any reporting there is an inherent bias just because it is done through our own eyes.

—CHARLAYNE HUNTER-GAULT

One cold Monday in January 1961, Charlayne Hunter drove from Atlanta to Athens, Georgia, to attend her first day of classes at the University of Georgia. The trip covered 75 miles (120 kilometers) of highway, but 250 years of history. It had taken two years of court battles and numerous delays, but persistence had won out. Charlayne Hunter was the first African-American woman admitted to this Southern school.

Her first days were scary. An angry mob gathered outside her dorm, shouting, jeering, and throwing bricks. One brick shattered her bedroom window, splattering glass over the clothing she was unpacking. She attended classes protected by federal marshals and followed by a pack of reporters. People stared and whispered about her. Even those students who didn't openly oppose her presence were afraid to speak to her.

Charlayne didn't enjoy being the subject of all those headlines. That's not why she had gone to college. She had gone to learn to write the headlines—to be a journalist, her dream since she was twelve years old. And that's what she did. After a while the novelty of her being at the university subsided and she went about the business of getting an education. Twenty-five years later, she was invited back as an honored guest to speak to the class of 1988 and to accept the George Foster Peabody Award, the highest honor a broadcast journalist can receive.

Charlayne was born in the tiny town of Due West, South Carolina. She spent most of her young years living with her mother and grandmother, both women of tremendous strength who helped to give Charlayne her determination. Charlayne's father, a chaplain in the army, wasn't home very often, but from him, Charlayne learned to think highly of herself and her abilities.

When Charlayne was five years old and too young to enter school, she went anyway. Most of her friends were a year older than she, so she simply followed them to school and took a seat in the back of the classroom. At the end of the year, she was promoted with her friends to second grade.

After moving several times, Charlayne, with her mother, grandmother, and two younger brothers settled in Atlanta. She edited her high school newspaper and wrote articles for a community weekly. Her role model was Brenda Starr, the ace reporter in a comic strip. When Charlayne told her guidance counselor she wanted to study journalism in college, the counselor told her that journalism was not meant for women, especially not black women. She suggested that Charlayne study teaching, a more attainable goal, but Charlayne was stubborn. She knew what she wanted and she was going after it one way or another. On her own, she scoured college catalogs searching for a journalism program and decided she'd have to leave the state to find it. No Georgia college offered journalism to African-American students.

Charlayne graduated from high school in 1959, a time when segregation of blacks and whites was standard and accepted throughout the South. Black people were allowed to ride only in the rear of buses. Signs for drinking fountains and rest rooms read "Colored" or "Whites." Blacks were not served in restaurants reserved for whites, did not attend the same churches as whites, and, of course, had separate schools.

When Charlayne began college, the civil rights movement had seen its first significant breakthroughs. In Alabama, Rosa Parks's refusal to give up her bus seat to a white man led to a significant protest led by Martin Luther King Jr., and in Arkansas, another high-profile protest resulted from nine African-American students attempting to attend the all-white Little Rock High School. But none of this had happened in Georgia, where Charlayne was trying to break similar barriers. She was soon approached by civil rights workers, who asked her if she would test the law in Georgia by applying to a Georgia university. Charlayne did apply, and as the legal battle over her application was fought in court, she attended Wayne State University in Detroit, Michigan.

In January 1961, she finally won her case and made her historic journey from Atlanta to Athens. Though at the beginning, she endured slurs and insults, she was eventually accepted as just another student. Shortly before she graduated, she married Walter Stovall, a white student with whom she later had a daughter. The marriage didn't last, but Charlayne and Walter remained friends. In 1971, she married again, this time to Ronald Gault, an African-American man from Chicago. She and Ron have a son.

After graduation, Charlayne took a secretarial job for *The New Yorker* magazine, where she was promoted to staff writer. She quickly gained a reputation as an excellent journalist and won many awards and citations. She later worked for the New York *Times* for nine years, where she headed the paper's Harlem Bureau, and did several investigative reports detailing the lives of poor African-American women.

Charlayne's first television job was anchoring the news on a local Washington, D.C., station. In 1978, she joined "The MacNeil-Lehrer Hour" on PBS, becoming the first African-American woman to anchor national news.

As a journalist, Charlayne has traveled the world covering stories. On the scene in South Africa, she interviewed blacks and whites about living

Charlayne Hunter-Gault on the scene in Africa

under apartheid, a system of strict separation of the races. This story resulted in one of her two Emmy Awards. The other was for a story about Agent Orange, a deadly poison sprayed in Vietnam to kill trees, but which made many people sick as well. In 1993, she was in the middle of the action during the United States invasion of Grenada.

Besides being a correspondent and news anchor, Charlayne has written for magazines such as *Vogue, Life, Ms.,* and *Essence.* She says she enjoys writing for magazines because it gives her a chance to express her own opinions, something she cannot do as a news reporter.

In June 1997, Charlayne left "The News Hour" and became the South Africa bureau chief for National Public Radio. When she delivers her reports, Charlayne is always very serious. She jokes that when people see her in person, they are surprised to see her smile and laugh. One of her favorite mementos is a framed New York *Times* crossword puzzle in which 38-Down asks for "the journalist who integrated U of Ga in 1961."

Annie **Leibovitz**

1949–
Photojournalist

When I say I want to photograph someone, what it really means is that I'd like to know them.

—ANNIE LEIBOVITZ

Most magazine and newspaper stories are accompanied by photographs, but most people don't know who took the pictures. Only the truly exceptional photographers become known to the general public. Annie Leibovitz, often called the most successful photographer of her generation, is one such exceptional photographer. Annie first came to the public's attention in the 1970s as the leading photographer for *Rolling Stone* magazine, taking photographs of the biggest rock stars of the era. Over the years, Annie has continued to photograph celebrities. She has developed her own unique style, often posing her famous subjects in unusual settings. For instance, she posed the African-American actress Whoopi Goldberg immersed in a tub full of white milk. And she photographed Roseanne and then-husband Tom Arnold slathered in mud. In 1991, a special collection representing twenty-five years of Annie's work was featured at the

National Portrait Gallery in Washington, D.C. Only once before had such a high tribute been paid to a living photographer.

Annie's photographs are unusual. But then, so are most aspects of Annie Leibovitz.

Annie was born in Westbury, Connecticut. Her father was a lieutenant colonel in the army, so much of Annie's childhood was spent on military bases around the world. At eighteen, she enrolled in the San Francisco Art Institute to study painting and enrolled in an evening photography course. After completing her freshman year, she flew to the Philippines to visit her parents and took a side trip to Japan, where she purchased her first camera.

During her junior year, Annie spent five months living on a *kibbutz* (a communal farm) in Israel as part of a student archaeological team excavating King Solomon's temple. In her spare time, she practiced her photography.

When she returned home, she wandered around San Francisco taking pictures of street people. It was then that the magic happened. Her boyfriend suggested she show her work to a new magazine dedicated to recording the counterculture of the 1970s. Annie took his advice. The magazine *Rolling Stone* went on to become the leading magazine of rock music, and Annie became its star photographer. One of her first cover shots was a portrait of the Beatles' John Lennon.

Annie felt that in order to do a good photo shoot, she had to become totally involved with her subjects. She followed the big rock groups on their tours across the country, living with, and becoming part of them. But sometimes she became too involved. Many of the rock stars of the 1970s were heavily into drugs, and Annie became addicted to cocaine. It took her five years to rid herself of the habit.

Annie remained with *Rolling Stone* for more than a decade. In 1983, Annie joined the staff of *Vanity Fair* magazine, where the celebrities she photographed included film stars, opera singers, and politicians. She also did freelance work, photographing highly visible and successful advertising posters for American Express credit cards and the Gap clothing chain.

Many of Annie's photographs were criticized as being improper and irreverent. One early photograph she had taken of John Lennon showed him nude next to his fully clothed wife, Yoko Ono. In 1991, her photograph of a very pregnant and unclothed Demi Moore on the cover of *Vanity Fair* shocked many readers. Annie explained that Ms. Moore was proud of the way she looked at that moment of her life and wanted to share her feelings with *Vanity Fair*'s readers. Though some people thought the picture in poor taste, others believed it was a sensitive and beautiful picture of a woman about to become a mother.

Annie works out of her large white studio, the walls of which are covered with a jumble of photographs of her friends, family, and famous people. Annie's professional work has appeared in publications and has been featured in gallery exhibits all over the world. The 1990s marked another change in Annie's career. She traveled to Sarajevo, where there were no celebrities and no staged poses, but only the pain of ordinary people caught in the crossfire of a brutal civil war in the former Yugoslavia. It has been said of Annie Leibovitz that she is a chronicler of her times. And that she is—from the rock culture of the 1970s, though the glamour stars of the 1980s, and the social upheavals of Eastern Europe in the 1990s.

Anna **Quindlen**

1953–
Syndicated Columnist

I think of a column as having a conversation with a person.

—ANNA QUINDLEN

Anna Quindlen, who began her journalism career in 1974, was lucky. She followed a path opened for her by those who had gone before. But it was on her own that she quickly became the star columnist who, in 1992, became one of the very few women to be awarded the Pulitzer Prize for commentary.

The oldest of five children, Anna grew up in a middle-class Catholic family. She was educated in Catholic schools by what she calls "liberal" nuns. Her brother remembers her as "focused," and she recalls always feeling the need to be perfect at anything she tried. In high school, she shouted encouragement for her team as a member of the cheerleading squad, edited the yearbook, and daydreamed of being married. She once said that the confidence everyone thought she had was a false front, and that she was really a pit of insecurities. She even admitted that as a teenager, she had more than once thought about suicide. "It was just too much pressure," she said.

When Anna was in college, her mother became ill with cancer, and Anna took a leave of absence to care for her and her four younger siblings. She later wrote of her mother's death, "I could never [again] look at life as anything but a great gift. I realized I didn't have any business taking it for granted."

Anna's climb to the top of her profession was rapid. Her success began early with a story published in *Seventeen* magazine when she was still in college. Just three years after graduating from Barnard College, she secured a job with the New York *Times*. Despite the *Times*'s reputation for being inhospitable to women, Anna was assigned to write one of the paper's important regular columns, "About New York." Not long after that, she became the deputy metropolitan editor. At this point in her career, though she was barely thirty years old, many people in the industry predicted that she would be in line for a full editorship.

But Anna, a woman who from her youth had been driven to push further and higher, wasn't content. She wanted more. She wanted to fulfill the ambition she had stated on her college application—to write the great American novel. She also wanted to spend more time with her two young sons, so she quit her job at the paper.

As she raised her children and worked on her novel, Anna found time to contribute occasional columns to the *Times*'s Home section. When her pieces in this column brought job offers from editors around the country, her boss at the *Times* enticed her with a feature column under her own name, "Life in the 30's." For two years, she shared her experiences as a young professional mother with her readers, but ended the column after her daughter was born because she didn't want to risk repeating herself. She was also afraid that something she wrote about her children might one day embarrass them.

Once again the *Times* was reluctant to let her go. They offered her a column on the editorial page, a spot traditionally reserved for men. This was a coup Anna could not turn down. In her column, "Public & Private," she wrote about controversial issues such as abortion, child care, the homeless, and often, her disagreements with the Catholic church.

This sharing of her own experiences and her down-to-earth reactions to them made her a favorite with readers. She used the same personal style in "Public & Private" that she had used in her earlier column, often using one individual's pain or triumph to illustrate a larger problem in society. Her goal was not to shape the opinions of her readers, but to help them shape their own. She says there are two kinds of columnists—those who tell you what to think and those who ask you to think. She said she hoped she was the second kind.

In 1994, after her second novel was published, Anna resigned from the *Times* for the second time to once again devote her time to writing fiction. Aside from her two novels, she has also written a children's picture book.

Christiane **Amanpour**

1958–
War Correspondent

Y ou spend the whole day watching people die, and there's just
no escape from it. It's so awful
that in the end you just can't describe it.
But I have to try. That's the job.

—CHRISTIANE AMANPOUR

Christiane Amanpour was still settling into her new post as CNN's foreign correspondent in Frankfurt, Germany. Within a few months of her arrival, the biggest story of the year began, but it wasn't happening in Germany. Saddam Hussein of Iraq ordered tanks and troops into the neighboring country of Kuwait. The Iraqis quickly stormed the capital, toppled the government, and claimed Kuwait as an extension of Iraq. The United Nations Security Council demanded Iraq's withdrawal, and the United States pledged to come to Kuwait's assistance if Iraq didn't withdraw.

Christiane did what journalists do. She hopped on a plane and was at Kuwait's border within hours. Over the next several months, as tensions in the area increased, Christiane kept CNN's international audience up to date on the explosive situation.

The deadline for Iraq's withdrawal came and went. Iraq held firm. The United States launched Operation Desert Storm. Christiane's face and her crisp British accent became familiar to millions of Americans who kept their television sets tuned to CNN all through the short but brutal Persian Gulf War.

Since the Gulf War, Christiane has became CNN's roving correspondent. Like most war correspondents, Christiane thrives on danger. She was the first international correspondent to provide concentrated coverage on the fierce struggle between the Moslems and the Serbs in Bosnia-Herzegovina. Her coverage of this war won her four of journalism's highest honors: the George Foster Peabody Award, the George Polk Memorial Award, the Alfred I. DuPont-Columbia University Silver Baton, and the 1994 Courage in Journalism Award presented by International Women's Media Foundation.

Since 1989, she has covered heart-wrenching stories of war in Rwanda and the rescue of thousands of starving children in Somalia. She was in Haiti when United States troops landed to prevent violence from erupting on that island. In fact, wherever violence erupts, Christiane is there, camera in hand, giving minute-by-minute reports.

Christiane was born in London, the oldest of four daughters of an Iranian businessman and a British mother. At that time, Iran was an oil-rich country run by the shah, who was friendly to the West. The Amanpours moved to Iran a few months after their daughter's birth. As a young child, Christiane enjoyed her family's position of wealth and prestige. When she was eleven years old, she and her sisters were sent to England to attend school. Christiane was unhappy and homesick. She had dreamed of one day becoming a doctor, but she was unable to get into medical school due to her poor grades.

Her initial decision to study journalism came about in a strange way. One of her sisters had been accepted by a journalism college in London, then changed her mind. The college refused to refund the tuition, so Christiane went in her sister's place.

Then, in 1979, Iran was thrown into turmoil. The shah of Iran was deposed by the Ayatollah Khomeini, a religious extremist who took over the country, and ended all relations with the West.

Christiane's parents returned to London, having to leave all their possessions and money behind. It was after this experience that Christiane decided she wanted to become a foreign correspondent. "If I was going to be affected by events, I wanted to be a part of them," she later said. She wanted to better understand why such things happened in the world and explain them to others.

She then came to the United States to continue her journalism studies at the University of Rhode Island. Shortly after her graduation in 1983, she applied for a position at CNN. Though Christiane began as an assistant, answering phones and typing scripts, she told everyone at the network she wanted to be a foreign correspondent. Her boss told her this was unlikely to happen, but Christiane said, "Just wait!"

During the summer of 1984, Christiane, on her own initiative, went to California to cover the Democratic National Convention. The following year, CNN did a special series on Iran. Christiane's Iranian background and knowledge helped to make that special a success. She was making herself a valuable member of the CNN team, and it wasn't long before she was rewarded with promotions that led to her appointment in Frankfurt.

It was largely Christiane's coverage of the Gulf War that catapulted CNN's ratings and made the network as successful as it is today. In fact, in the wake of CNN's phenomenal success, the regular networks have changed their news formats to include more frequent updates of breaking news and round-the-clock coverage for big stories.

Today Christiane lives in Paris and chooses assignments that take her around the world. She is a powerful and influential member of the news community since her choices determine what CNN viewers watch. This power was clearly demonstrated with her coverage of the war in Bosnia and Herzegovina. Until Christiane's intense coverage of this struggle, the rest of the world had paid little attention to it.

Christiane Amanpour

Christiane adds her personal perspective to the news she covers by doing poignant, heartbreaking stories on the suffering that war inflicts on innocent people. In Bosnia, she did not hesitate to state publicly that the Bosnian government was the aggressor, and many people criticized her for not maintaining journalistic objectivity. And, because of her stance, Bosnia refused to allow her to enter their territory. She said, "I only report what I see. What does it mean to be completely unbiased? If I were covering the Holocaust, would I have to say, 'Oh, the poor Nazis, maybe they have a point.'?"

Christiane has earned a reputation for both intelligent reporting and bravery. Within only ten years, she has risen to the top of her profession and has won several awards for her work. Because of her immense popularity with viewers, other networks would like to have her on their teams. In 1994, she considered switching to another network, but elected to stay with CNN, at a reported salary of nearly a million dollars a year.

Asked about her own status as one of only a few women war correspondents, Christiane acknowledges the debt she owes to her predecessors. "Women before me have forged the path," she said. She also feels being a woman is an advantage because, "People open up to you more than they would to a man."

APPENDIX

Sixty-Four Other Extraordinary Women Journalists

Charlotte Spears Bass (1880–1969) Editor of the California *Eagle*, the oldest African-American paper on the West Coast; an early advocate of civil rights.

Bessie Beattie (1886–1947) Writer, editor, and all-around journalist. One of the first women radio commentators. Covered the Russian Revolution from Russia for *Good Housekeeping* magazine.

Anna Benjamin (1874–1902) The first woman war correspondent to travel with the fighting forces. Covered wars in Cuba, the Philippines, Russia, and Japan.

Winifred Black Bonfils (1863–1936) Wrote under the pen name Annie Laurie; newspaper reporter who was a society editor, a drama critic, a city editor, a managing editor, a foreign correspondent, and a syndicated columnist, and did important investigative reporting in Chicago, New York, and Texas.

Therese Bonney (1894–1978) Photojournalist known for her "truth raids," in which she documented the effects of war on the small villages and towns of Europe. Her photography was showcased in one-woman shows at the Library of Congress, the Museum of Modern Art, and many European museums.

Heloise Bowles (1919–1977) Originated "Hints from Heloise" household-advice column in 1962.

Mildred Alice Edie Brady (1906–1965) An early consumer advocate, she organized the Western Consumer Union in 1938 and was editor of *Consumer Reports* magazine from 1958 to 1964.

Cheryl Brownstein-Santiago (1951–) Editor for Los Angeles *Times* Spanish-language edition. A leader in promoting the careers of Hispanic-American journalists.

Leonel Ross Campbell (1857–1938) Better known as "Polly Pry." Most of her career was based in Denver, Colorado, but she also reported from around the world. Published her own magazine, *Polly Pry*.

Mary Shadd Cary (1823–1893) A free-born African-American who moved to Canada and established a school for black refugees fleeing the United States. She was the first black woman in North America to publish and edit a weekly newspaper, the *Provincial Freeman*.

Edna Woolman Chase (1877–1957) Editor of *Vogue* magazine from 1914 to 1948. Set the pace for fashion news in the United States and staged the country's first fashion show in 1914.

Connie Chung (1946–) Star news reporter for NBC for almost twenty years who became co-anchor of the "CBS Evening News" in 1993. She was only the second woman to anchor a television network's nightly news program.

Katie Couric (1957–) Co-host of NBC's "Today" show since 1991. Considered one of the top broadcast journalists of the present day.

Elizabeth May Craig (1889–1975) Wrote an important political column, "Inside Washington," for forty years and was a panelist on NBC's "Meet the Press." An ardent and active proponent of women's rights who took part in the suffragist demonstration at President Woodrow Wilson's inauguration.

Heloise Ponce Cruise (1951–) Daughter of the original "Heloise" who took over the "Hints from Heloise" column after her mother died. Today, the column is syndicated to hundreds of papers in several countries and "Heloise" has authored several best-selling books.

Elizabeth Mapes Dodge (1831–1905) Author of classic children's story *Hans Brinker and the Silver Skates*, wrote for *Atlantic Monthly* and *Harper's* magazine. For many years, editor of *St. Nicholas*, the leading children's magazine of the nineteenth century.

Mary Abigail Dodge (1833–1896) Wrote pro-abolition and anti-women's suffrage articles under pen name "Gail Hamilton" for the *Atlantic Monthly* and many other leading magazines.

Maureen Dowd (1952–) Editorial columnist for the New York *Times* since 1995. Considered by many to be one of the top columnists of the 1990s.

Linda Ellerbee (1944–) A veteran television journalist who now focuses on producing children's news and informational television programming.

Katherine Woodruff Fanning (1927–) Won a Pulitzer Prize as owner/publisher of the Anchorage *Daily*. Also edited the *Christian Science Monitor* from 1983 to 1988.

Janet Flanner (1892–1978) Moved from the United States to Paris in the 1920s and served as a political columnist for *The New Yorker* for close to fifty years.

Doris Fleeson (1901–1970) A police reporter in New York, a war correspondent during World War II, and after the war was the first syndicated woman political columnist based in Washington, D.C. Helped found the American Newspaper Guild.

Pauline Frederick (1909–1990) The first woman television network correspondent to cover a national political convention; the first woman to moderate a debate between presidential candidates (1976); and the first woman to win the Peabody and DuPont broadcasting awards.

Toni Frissell (1907–1988) Photojournalist during World War II whose coverage of WACS (the women's military division) and of an African-American fighter pilots regiment helped change Americans' attitudes about the ability of women and blacks as effective military personnel.

Ellen Holta Goodman (1941–) Syndicated columnist currently carried in several hundred daily newspapers. Won Pulitzer Prize for social commentary in 1980.

Lorena Hickock (1893–1968) A close friend of Franklin and Eleanor Roosevelt, she covered Roosevelt's 1932 campaign, helping to open the way for women to cover political news. First advised Eleanor Roosevelt to hold weekly news conferences open only to women journalists.

Molly Ivins (1945–) Syndicated columnist who was given the Lifetime Achievement Award by the National Society of Newspaper Columnists in 1994.

Alice May Lee Jemison (1901–1964) Publisher of the *First American*, the United States' first Native American newsletter. A leader in the campaign for Native American causes.

Freda Kirchwey (1893–1976) Editor of *Nation* magazine from 1932 to 1955; a leader in the peace and disarmament movements.

Gertrude Lane (1874–1941) Editor of *Woman's Home Companion*, a popular magazine in the 1930s that featured many writers who later became best-selling authors.

Dorothy Lange (1895–1965) One of the earliest women photojournalists. Best known for her documentary photographs of the Depression era and of Japanese-Americans interned in camps during World War II.

Sara Jane Clark Lippincott (1823–1904) Known better as Grace Greenwood. One of the first women to write a syndicated column based in Washington, D.C. Edited one of the country's earliest children's magazines, *Young Pilgrim*. As editor, published new writers such as Louisa May Alcott, Longfellow, and Whittier.

Clara Littledale (1891–1956) One of the first women journalists to work out of the city room of the New York *Evening Post*. Editor of *Good Housekeeping* and *Parents* magazines for several years.

Clare Booth Luce (1903–1987) Journalist, playwright, novelist, diplomat, and politician. Editor of *Vogue* and *Vanity Fair* and a member of Congress from 1943 to 1947. Recipient of the Presidential Medal of Honor in 1983.

Marya Mannes (1940–1990) Editor of popular magazines such as *Vogue* and *Glamour* for many years and a columnist for *McCall's*. Also host of early TV program, "I Speak for Myself."

Marie Manning (Beatrice Fairfax) (1873–1945) One of the first nationally known advice columnists, popular during the first half of the twentieth century.

Mary Ellen Mark (1940–) Photojournalist best known for her photographs of social commentary.

Judith Martin (1938–) Syndicated columnist known as "Miss Manners." Has replaced Emily Post as the guru of proper etiquette and polite behavior.

Sarah McClendon (1910–) Pioneer woman journalist and investigative reporter. Currently a White House correspondent for more than five decades.

Agnes Meyers (1887–1970) Mother of Washington *Post* publisher Katherine Graham. Writer for the *Post* for many years, championing social causes.

Eleanor Packard (1905–1972) Pilot and war correspondent in World War II.

Alicia Patterson (1906–1963) New York *Newsday* writer who won a Pulitzer Prize in 1954. Niece of Eleanor Patterson.

Eleanor (Cissy) Medill Patterson (1881–1948) Editor and publisher of the Washington *Herald*. One of first women to edit and publish a major newspaper.

Jane Pauley (1950–) One of the leading women television journalists of the 1980s and 1990s. Longtime association with NBC News has included years as co-host of the "Today" show and currently the newsmagazine show "Dateline."

Ethel Payne (1911–1991) Pioneering African-American reporter who covered Washington politics and all the major events of the civil rights movement during the 1950s and 1960s.

Sylvia Porter (1913–1991) Author of syndicated consumer-advice column "Your Money's Worth," which ran for more than forty years. Her 1976 book *Sylvia Porter's Money Book* was on the best-seller list for years.

Emily Post (1873–1960) Syndicated columnist who was long considered the last word on proper etiquette.

Ishbell Ross (1895–1975) Considered one of the best women reporters of the 1920s. In 1936, wrote the influential book *Ladies of the Press*, which was considered the major reference work for women in journalism up to that time.

Aline Saarinen (1914–1972) Began her career as an art critic, but went on to become one of the first women foreign correspondents for television. She headed the NBC News Bureau in Paris.

Jessica Savitch (1948–1983) Rose quickly from local news reporting to national prominence as the "golden girl" of NBC News. Automobile accident took her life at the peak of her career.

Diane Sawyer (1942–) Star television journalist for ABC News. Co-host of ABC's "Prime Time Live."

Dorothy Schiff (1903–1989) Owner/publisher of the New York *Post* for close to forty years, one of the longest-lasting papers in the country.

Ellen Browning Scripps (1836–1932) With her brother, helped found what grew into the Scripps-Howard chain of newspapers. After retiring from her career as a journalist, she became a philanthropist and founded several schools.

Agnes Smedley (1892–1950) Foreign correspondent who was a known supporter of Chinese Communism. Accused of being a spy during both world wars, but none of the charges were ever proven.

Hazel Smith (1914–1994) Editor of a small Mississippi newspaper who wrote about civil rights issues. The first woman to win a Pulitzer Prize.

Leslie Stahl (1941–) One of the first newswomen on television and one of the best-respected women television journalists.

Hannah Storm (1963–) Television sports journalist who became the first woman to host a major American sports championship telecast when she covered the 1997 NBA Finals on NBC.

Helen Thomas (1920–) Known as the First Lady of White House reporting. Has covered the White House since the 1960s.

Nina Totenberg (1944–) Featured newscaster on NPR and an expert on the Supreme Court and Washington legal affairs.

Judith Viorst (1931–) Columnist for *Redbook* magazine, novelist, and author of children's books *Alexander and the Terrible, Horrible, No-Good Day*.

Mary Heaton Vorse (1874–1966) Wrote books and magazine articles focusing on labor issues.

Linda Werthheimer (1943–) Radio journalist who helped to pioneer NPR news.

Judy Woodruff (1946–) White House correspondent for decades. Joined CNN in 1993 and co-anchors "Inside Politics" and "The World Today."

Anna Zenger (1704–1751) With her husband, owned and published a weekly journal in colonial New York. Continued to publish the paper while her husband was jailed for libel after printing uncomplimentary articles about the British. The Zengers are considered important for establishing precedents of freedom of the press in America.

GLOSSARY

ABC (American Broadcasting Companies, Inc.)
major broadcast television and radio network

almanac
book published every year that lists a variety of facts and figures, including outstanding events, weather information, and movements of heavenly bodies

anthology
a collection of writings from different sources

byline
line at the beginning of a news story giving the author's name

CBS (Columbia Broadcast System)
major broadcast television and radio network

CNN (Cable News Network)
cable television network that broadcasts only news and current-events programming

commercial broadcasting
television or radio stations and networks (such as NBC or ABC) that attempt to make a profit by charging fees for commercial advertising during programming

compositor

person who "sets type," or places letters on a printing press

cub reporter

young, inexperienced reporter

documented

proven true by evidence such as printed documents

editor

person in charge of certain aspects of publishing books, newspapers, or magazines; assigns reporters to cover certain stories, checks stories for accuracy

editorial

statement of opinion printed by a newspaper or magazine (unlike regular news stories, which are statements of fact)

exposé

article that reveals facts or rumors damaging to the subject

feminist

person who believes in and fights for equal rights for women

filler

short news stories used to fill up empty space in a newspaper

freelancer

worker who is paid for a specific job, such as a news article, upon its completion (unlike full-time employees who are paid a steady salary for working daily)

ghost writer
a person who writes a book or article that is published under the name of another writer

hearsay
facts that could be doubtful because they are based on rumor rather than on a firsthand witness's account

intellectual
person whose main activity is to study and to develop ideas

masthead
the portion of the newspaper that displays the paper's name

muckraker
reporter who searches for and reveals secrets and rumors about public figures

NAACP (National Association for the Advancement of Colored People)
major civil rights organization

NBC (National Broadcasting Company)
major broadcast television and radio network

NPR (National Public Radio)
not-for-profit radio network partially funded by the federal government

obituary
public notice of a person's death, usually accompanied by a brief biography

pamphlet

a brief, informational publication that is not bound like a book

PBS (Public Broadcasting Service)

non-profit television network partially funded by the federal government

proofread

to carefully read a manuscript and correct errors of grammar, spelling, and punctuation

public broadcasting

television and radio stations (such as NPR and PBS) that do not profit from commercial advertising and are partially funded by the federal government

publisher

person who is in charge of an entire publishing company and oversees all the editors and writers

Pulitzer Prize

annual award that are among the highest honors awarded to journalists

scoop

to discover certain facts and be the first to publish them

sensationalize

to arouse readership (in newspapers or magazines) or viewership (in television) by emphasizing lurid, violent, sexually explicit, or scandalous news stories

serial (or serialized)

a story published in several parts (or chapters) over time

suffrage
the right to vote

syndicate
a group or network of businesses linked together

typesetting
placing letters and pictures in a form so that they can be printed

For Further Information

Books for Younger Readers

Ayer, Eleanor. *Margaret-Bourke White: Photographer for the World.* Dillon, 1992.

Blumberg, Rose. *Bloomers! (Amelia Bloomer).* Bradbury, 1994.

Carlson, Judy. *"Nothing is Impossible," Said Nellie Bly.* Raintree-Steck Vaughn, 1992.

Cousins, Margaret. *Ben Franklin of Old Philadelphia.* Random House, 1987 (1952).

Cousins, Margaret. *The Story of Thomas Alva Edison.* Random House, 1981 (1965).

Cullen-Dupont, Kathryn. *Elizabeth Cady Stanton & Women's Liberty.* Facts on File, 1992

Daffron, Carolyn. *Gloria Steinem: Feminist.* Chelsea House, 1988.

English, Betty L. *Women at Their Work.* Pied Piper Books, 1988.

Freedman, Suzanne. *Ida B. Wells-Barnett and the Antilynching Crusade.* Millbrook, 1994.

Harvey, Miles. *Women's Voting Rights.* Children's Press, 1996.

Hayes, Richard. *Ida B Wells: Antilynching Crusader and American Troublemaker.* Raintree-Steck Vaughn, 1994.

Hoff, Mark. *Gloria Steinem: The Women's Movement.* Millbrook, 1984.

Kendall, Martha E. *Nellie Bly: Reporter for the World.* Millbrook, 1992.

McKissack, Pat. *Ida B Wells-Barnett: Voice Against Violence.* Enslow, 1994.

Quackenbush, Robert. *Stop the Presses: Nellie's Got a Scoop.* Simon Schuster, 1992.

Read, Phyllis J. and Bernard L. Whitlieb. *The Book of Women's Firsts.* Random House, 1992.

Smith, Betsy, C. *Women Win the Vote.* Silver Burdett Press, 1989.

Sullivan, George. *The Day the Women Got the Vote, A Photo History of the Women's Rights Movement.* Scholastic, 1994

Books for Older Readers

Bourke-White, Margaret. *Portrait of Myself.* Simon & Schuster, 1963.

Colwell, Lynn Hunter. *Erma Bombeck: Humor Columnist.* Enslow, 1992.

Cush, Cathy. *Women Who Achieved Greatness.* Raintree Steck-Vaughn, 1994.

Daffron, Carolyn. *Margaret Bourke-White: Photographer.* Chelsea House, 1988.

Davidson, Sue. *Getting the Real Story: Nellie Bly and Ida B. Wells.* Seal Press, 1992.

Downs, Robert B. and Jane B. *Journalists of the United States: Biographical Sketches of Print and Broadcast News Shapers from the Late 17th Century to the Present.* McFarland & Co., 1991.

Emerson, Karen, L. *Nellie Bly — Making Headlines: A Biography of Nellie Bly.* Dillon, 1989.

Evans, Sara M. *Born for Liberty: A History of Women in America.* The Free Pess, 1989.

Falkoff, Lucille. *Helen Gurley Brown: Queen of Cosmo.* Garnett, 1992.

Geyer, Georgia Ann. *Buying the Night Flight.* Dell Publishing, 1983.

Ivins, Molly. *Molly Ivins Can't Say That, Can She?* Random House, 1992.

Kunstadter, Marie. *Women Working A–Z.* Highsmith Press, 1994.

Lent, John A., *Women and Mass Communications: An International Annotated Bibliography.* Greenwood, 1991.

Lont, Cynthia M., *Women & Media: Content, Careers, and Criticism.* Wadsworth Pub., 1995.

Malone, Mary. *Barbara Walters: TV Superstar.* Enslow, 1990.

Malone, Mary. *Connie Chung: Broadcast Journalist.* Enslow, 1992.

Rubenstein, David. *Before the Suffragettes: Women's Emancipation in the 1890s.* St. Martin's Press, 1986.

Sagan, Miriam. *Women's Suffrage.* Lucent Books, 1995.

Smith, Lucinda. *Women Who Write: From Past and Present to Future*. Silver Burdett Press, 1989.

Smith, Lucinda. *Women Who Write II*. Simon & Schuster, 1994.

Stephens, Mitchell. *A History of the News: From the Drum to the Satellite*. Viking, 1988.

Wollstonecraft, Mary. *Vindication of the Rights of Women*. Alfred A. Knopf, 1992 (reprint).

Organizations and Internet Sites of Interest

"20/20"
http://www.abcnews.com/onair/2020/html_files/index.html
Home page for the ABC television news magazine "20/20" co-hosted by **Barbara Walters.**

American Journalism Historians Association
c/o Don Avery
Eastern Connecticut State University
83 Windham Street
Willimantic, Connecticut 06226
An organization that studies American and international media history.

Black Women in Publishing (BWIP)
10 E. 87th Street
New York, New York 10128
An organization that works to provide information, encouragement, and support to those who are interested in publishing, writing, and marketing books, magazines, and newspapers.

Cokie Roberts
http://www.abcnews.com/onair/thisweek/
A biography of **Cokie Roberts,** plus information about the ABC news show on which she appears, "This Week."

Distinguished Women of Past and Present
http://www.netsrq.com:80/~dbois/
Website that provides biographies of famous female writers, educators, scientists, heads of state, politicians, civil rights crusaders, artists, and entertainers.

Liz Smith
http://www.newsday.com/mainnews/lizsmith.htm
A New York *Newsday* site that features gossip columnist **Liz Smith's** daily column.

Ms. Foundation for Women (MFW)
120 Wall Street, 33rd Floor
New York, New York 10005
An organization that supports women and girls who take control of their own lives and influence the world around them.

Ms. Magazine
http://www.womweb.com/msnet.htm
Homepage for *Ms.*, the magazine founded by **Gloria Steinem.**

Molly Ivins
http://www.arlington.net/today/news/opinions/columntext/ivins2.htm
Fort Worth *Star-Telegram* page that contains **Molly Ivins's** column.

National Organization for Women (NOW)
1000 16th Street N.W., Suite 700
Washington, D.C. 20036
e-mail: now@now.org
http://www.now.org/now/
Organization of men and women whose common goal is to end discrimination against women in government, industry, the workplace, church, political parties, science, education and medicine.

National Public Radio (NPR)
http://www.npr.org/
In addition to the latest news, find information on **Linda Wertheimer** and other top women journalists.

National Women and Media Collection
University of Missouri
School of Journalism
Columbia, Missouri 65211
e-mail: whmc@ext.missouri.edu
http://www.system.missouri.edu/whmc/womedia.htm
An organization that provides information about women's roles in the media industry. Also explains how these roles and the attitudes about women have changed.

National Woman's Party
Sewall-Belmont House
144 Constitution Ave., NE
Washington, D.C. 20002
This organization maintains the NWP Equal Rights and Suffrage Art Gallery in the Sewall-Belmont house in Washington, D.C. The museum is a national landmark filled with memorabilia relating to the struggle for women's right to vote.

National Women's History Project (NWHP)
7738 Bell Road
Windsor, California 95492
e-mail: NWHP@aol.com
http://qqq.nwhp.org
An organization dedicated to promoting awareness of women's history.
Sponsors annual National Women's History month.

NBC News
http://www.msnbc.com/
Home page that features several leading women broadcast journalists,
including **Jane Pauley.**

Newswomen's Club of New York (NCNY)
15 Gramercy Park South
New York, NY 10003
A group of women journalists who work full-time or freelance for New
York City daily newspapers, magazines, and radio and television stations.

U-Express
http://www.uexpress.com/ups/
The website for United Press Syndicate, which carries many of the
nation's leading columnists. Find a direct link to Dear Abby's **(Abigail
Van Buren)** daily column, and the index provides a link to an archive of
many columns by **Mary McGrory.**

Women Come to the Front
http://www/ibd.nrc.ca/
A website that provides information about female journalists, photographers, and broadcasters during World War II.

Women's Feature Service
http://www.womensnet.org/wfs/
Internet network of women journalists from forty countries in regions all over the world.

Women's Hall of Fame
http://www.rust.net/~cbledsoe/resource/promwom.htm#fame
Website that provides information about women who have made significant contributions to our society.

Women's Institute for Freedom of the Press (WIFP)
3306 Ross Place N.W.
Washington, D.C. 20008-3332
e-mail: wifponline@igc.apc.prg
http://www.igc.org/wifp/
A group concerned with the expansion of women's media outreach to the public.

INDEX

ERA (Equal Rights Amendment), 211–212

Everybody's Magazine, 109

Fairfax, Beatrice. *See* Manning, Marie

Fanning, Katherine Woodruff, 239

Fanny Fern. *See* Parton, Sara Payson Willis

Farm and Fireside, 151

Feminine Mystique, 210

Fern Leaves from Fanny's Port-Folio, 37

Field, Kate, 72–74

First American, 241

Five Fifteen, 100

Flanner, Janet, 240

Fleeson, Doris, 240

food columnists, 150–152

foreign correspondents, 34, 137–140, 142–143, 204–208, 232–235

Fortune, 154–155

Frank Leslie's Chimney Corner, 64

Frank Leslie's Lady's Journal, 64

Frank Leslie's Popular Monthly, 65–66

Franklin, Benjamin, 17–18

Frederick, Pauline, 240

Free Speech, 95

freedom of the press, 25, 245

Friedan, Betty, 210

Frissell, Toni, 240

Fugitive Slave Law, 52

Fuller, Margaret, 40

General Federation of Women's Clubs, 61

Geyer, Georgie Anne, 204–208

ghost writing, 159–160

Gilmer, Elizabeth Meriwether (Dorothy Dix), 77, 86

Glamour, 241

Goddard, Mary Katherine, 20–22

Goddard, Sarah Updike, 19–21

Godey's Lady's Book, 28–31, 40, 52, 61

Good Housekeeping, 147, 158–159, 237, 241

Good Morning America (ABC), 197

Goodman, Ellen Holta, 240

Göring, Hermann, 137–138

gossip columnists, 116–124, 192–194

Graham, Katharine Meyer, 166–170

Graham, Sheilah, 121–124

Great Depression, 155, 189

Hale, Sarah Josepha Buell, 27–31, 40, 44

PHOTO CREDITS

Photographs ©: AP/Wide World Photos: 2, 7, 8, 100, 133, 137, 150, 175, 180; Archive Photos: 5, 6, 27, 63, 67, 70, 120; Brown Brothers: 6, 86; Capital Cities/ABC, Inc.: back cover, right, 8, 199, 217; Courtesy of Charlayne Hunter-Gault: 224; Claire Price-Groff: 8, 204; Corbis-Bettmann: 5, 17, 32, 41, 42; Cosmopolitan: back cover, right, 8, 189; Culver Pictures: 7, 125, 146, 161; Gamma-Liaison: 9, 226 (Steve Morgan); Courtesy of Georgie A. Geyer: 206; Globe Photos: 8, 192 (Henry McGee), 8, 195 (Donald Sanders), 8, 213 (Adam Scull), 9, 229 (Walter Weissman); Courtesy The Historic New Orleans Collection: 6, 75; The Historical Society of Pennsylvania: 5, 6, 36, 72; Library of Congress: 5, 6, 45, 55, 57, 107; Margaret Bourke-White /Life Magazine © Time Inc.: 157; MacNeil/Lehrer Productions: back cover, right, 9, 221 (Christopher Little); Magnum Photos: 9, 232 (Luc Delahaye); New York Public Library, Schomburg Center for Research in Black Culture: 92; North Wind Picture Archives: 29, 65; Paul Lee/Best Efforts Inc.: cover, 6, 90; The Rhode Island Historical Society: 5, 20; Sophia Smith Collection, Smith College, Northampton, MA: 5, 50, 59; Underwood & Underwood/Corbis-Bettmann: 6, 82; UPI/Corbis-Bettmann: cover inset, back cover, left, 5, 6, 7, 8, 46, 48, 97, 98, 99, 101, 105, 112, 117, 118, 122, 127, 129, 141, 153, 164, 166, 184, 186, 202; Walter P. Calahan: 219; Courtesy of the Washington Post: 8, 171.

About the Author

One of Claire Price-Groff's childhood ambitions was to be a journalist. Perhaps if she had been aware of the many other women who did become journalists she would have pursued this goal more vigorously. She did not become a journalist, but did become a high school English teacher, which she enjoyed for many years. Now Ms. Price-Groff writes books for young people.

She grew up in Massachusetts, but has lived in Florida for many years with her husband and her little black dog.